TURNING MEMBERS INTO
LEADERS

TURNING MEMBERS INTO
LEADERS

How to raise up
your group members
to lead new groups

DR. DAVE EARLEY

Cell Group Resources™, a division of TOUCH® Outreach Ministries
Houston, Texas, U.S.A.

Published by Cell Group Resources™
P.O. Box 7847
Houston, Texas, 77270, U.S.A.
800-735-5865

Cover design by Don Bleyl

Text design by Rick Chandler

Editing by Scott Boren

All Scripture quotations, unless otherwise indicated, are from the Holy Bible, New International Version, Copyright © 1973, 1978, 1984 by International Bible Society. Used by permission.

Cell Group Resources™ is a book publishing division of TOUCH® Outreach Ministries, a resource and consulting ministry for churches with a vision for cell-based local church structure.

www.touchusa.org

CONTENTS

FOREWORD

Many small group books on the market focus on how to have the perfect group experience. Few, however, explain why small groups are the perfect breeding ground for future leaders. This is one of those rare books.

When Christ saw the burgeoning needs around him, He said to His disciples, " … Ask the Lord of the harvest, therefore, to send out workers into his harvest field" (Mt. 9:36-38). Churches do not reap the harvest because they have small groups. They reap the harvest because they have harvest workers. Unless small group members are converted into small group leaders, little long-term fruit remains.

Dave Earley understands this principle. The church he started in 1985 has grown to about 2000 people with over 125 small groups.

Dr. Earley's first book, *Eight Habits of Effective Small Group Leaders* revealed the habits of great small group leadership. This book, *Turning Members into Leaders,* gives practical advice on how to convert small group members into effective leaders.

In this book you'll learn how to dream for a multitude of leaders, model effective leadership, explain the vision with clarity, and how to release a new generation of leaders. The book will help you and your church fulfill the Great Commission by identifying, developing, and releasing your current members into small group leaders who reap the harvest.

Joel Comiskey

INTRODUCTION:
THE DETERMINING FACTOR

I was a very young man when I planted a church. I think I'm still young, but no one else does. We planted with a team of young couples who all had full-time jobs in the community. After about a year of hard work and seeing our church grow from 12 to 150, I reached the end of my limits.

Then an idea began to dawn on me. The key to this church's future wasn't the ministry I could do or even we as a church planting team could do. The key to our church's future would be the ministry we could raise up *others* to do. I discovered that leadership development is the determining factor for maximum impact.

Anyone who has desired to make a deep, broad, lasting impact has come to the same conclusion. After eighteen years as the senior pastor of the church we planted in 1985, I keep coming back to the same conclusion. Leadership development is the determining factor. Of course I'm not alone in expressing this crying need for leadership. Listen to what George Barna has said,

> I have spent the last 15 years researching all facets of American life … Some have said I am obsessive about having information before making a judgment … Now after fifteen years of diligent digging into the world around me, I reached several conclusions regarding the future of the Christian Church in America. The central conclusion is that the American church is dying due to a lack of strong leadership … Nothing is more important than leadership.[1]

Nothing is more important than leadership. First we must become effective leaders. Then we must develop effective leaders.

Dale Galloway said it this way,

> From 1972 to 1995 I had the joy of pioneering what many have called one of the most effective small group systems in North America. We experienced big things in small groups. Thousands were brought to Christ, then effectively discipled and cared for in small groups. In retrospect the one thing we did that was the most outstanding was develop hundreds of leaders. If you build leaders, they will build cell groups and through them the church.[2]

Notice he said, *"The thing we did that was most outstanding was developing hundreds of leaders."* Leadership development is the determining factor.

Russ Robinson and Bill Donahue, who oversaw a network of 2,700 groups, made this point, "An emerging small group ministry cannot succeed without a commitment to effective leadership development ... A small group ministry rises and falls on the quality of its leaders."[3] Everything—including and especially a small group ministry—rises and falls on the quality of its leaders.

Joel Comiskey, the outstanding author and researcher of high impact cell ministry around the world, gets to the point:

> I have researched small groups around the world. Here's what I have discovered: Small groups are not the answer ... Small groups come and go, they rise and fall over time. Unless small group members are converted into small group leaders, little long-term fruit remains. Churches do not reap the harvest because they have small groups. They reap the harvest because they have harvest workers. Churches that have no plan to develop leaders have by default, planned to lose the harvest.[4]

If leadership is the determining factor, why do few small group leaders effectively multiply themselves by developing effective leaders? I believe it's because, even though most small group leaders have a passion to be used of God to raise up effective leaders, they're not sure how to do it. They need a practical strategy to make it happen.

I've spent the last twenty years on a quest to learn *how* to mentor and multiply effective leaders. I started with the disciple-making ministry of Jesus. I then studied the multiplying ministry of Barnabas into the life of Paul. I also read everything I could find on disciple making, leadership development and cell ministry. I attended many seminars and listened to more tapes than I can count. I talked with effective pastors and Christian leaders. And I experimented.

I've come to see the eight steps Jesus used for developing effective leaders reinforced again and again in ministry experience. I've taught these eight steps for developing leaders to hundreds of pastors, Christian leaders, missionaries, and small group leaders.

I believe these eight steps will help anyone interested in mentoring and multiplying effective leaders. Some of the reasons are:

1. The eight steps are biblical. They were practiced by both Jesus in his disciple-making ministry and Barnabas in helping develop Paul for ministry.

2. The eight steps are universal. They apply to all cultures and all types of groups. They're simple universal steps that will work for any type of group and any type of leader. I'm currently training 14-year-old students to practice them.

They're usable with any group of people, whatever their age, race, gender, or socioeconomic level. They can be lived in the inner city or on the farm. They work for those on a college campus, those in a foreign nation, and those in the suburbs of the United States.

Although some see a distinction between "small groups" and "cell groups," in this book the terms are treated interchangeably. This is because the eight steps are universal and apply to both. One beautiful fact is that they're essentially the same habits that apply to developing any type of leader. They can be used to mentor and multiply coaches of small group leaders, zone directors, small group pastors, and church planters. Once a leader incorporates them, he or she has the foundation for moving up the levels of small group leadership and kingdom impact.

3. The eight steps are effective. Following the eight steps for multiplying small leaders can make all the difference between mediocrity and greatness, between faithfulness and fruitfulness, between stagnation and multiplication. Following them can produce future leaders and will multiply your ministry.

4. The eight steps are simple. They're easy to understand and remember. I've seen leaders' eyes light up, and the light bulb of recognition turn on as the eight steps are explained.

5. The eight steps are practical. You can use them. Any leader can put them into practice, if they'll invest the time. When the steps are explained, leaders nod and say things like, "This is just what I've been looking for. Now I have a clear course to follow. I can do this." They're realistic expectations. Most leaders can fit them into their busy schedules.

It doesn't take a spiritual giant or someone with unlimited time to do them. These eight steps are attainable goals for small group leaders.

6. The eight steps are vital. Leadership development is the determining factor. The ability to successfully develop leaders will determine such vital issues as the size, strength, and health of your ministry. It will predict the excellence of your ministry and its long-term impact/future. Developing leaders is the only way to develop the speed and flexibility required for your ministry to handle change. Multiplying leaders is the only way we can ever hope to fulfill the Great Commission and reap the harvest

7. The eight steps are motivating. Upon learning them, leaders burn with the passion to put them into practice. The eight steps are challenging but not overwhelming.

The eight steps for multiplying leaders provide a track to take a small group leader, and those under him or her, to a new level. Whether an apprentice to a small group leader, a novice small group leader, a seasoned leader, a coach of small group leaders, a director of a district of groups, the pastor of a large small-groups ministry, or the pastor of a small church, the eight steps will work. These steps serve as a path that leads to fruitfulness and multiplication. The eight steps will help leaders, and those under them, experience greater fulfillment in ministry.

Eight Steps for Developing New Small Group Leaders

DREAM: Dream of Multiplying Leaders.
DEMONSTRATE: Demonstrate Multiplying Leadership.
DISCOVER: Discover Potential Leaders.
DEEPEN: Deepen Your Relationship with Them.
DESCRIBE: Describe the Vision to Them.
DETERMINE: Determine the Commitments to be Made.
DEVELOP: Develop Them for Leadership.
DEPLOY: Deploy Them into Leadership.

DREAM:

Dream of the Difference You Can Make by Multiplying Effective Leaders

To meet him, you wouldn't be aware of the impact he has had, is having, and will have. The first time we met, Scott introduced himself to me as "just a pizza shop guy." Yet, he soon received some training and began to lead a small group in our church. He worked hard and his group grew.

> The first step for developing new group leaders is to dream of mentoring healthy, growing, multiplying leaders.

Then Scott caught the dream of multiplication. Soon he had trained Mark to lead a group. Then he trained Dale. Then he trained Steve. In ten years, he trained four group leaders out of his group! On top of that, another young man he mentored will soon be planting a church. Scott has made quite an impact for "just a pizza shop guy." It began when he caught the dream of making a difference by multiplying leaders.

A Big Dream Makes a Big Difference

In 1987, Cesar Fajardo had a small ministry with only thirty young people in his youth group. Yet, he had a big dream. He took a photograph of the nearby indoor soccer stadium, and then hung the picture on the wall of his room. He began to dream and believe that God would one day fill it with young people. Today 18,000 young people line up on Saturday nights to get inside that stadium for his youth worship service.

Within twelve years he had raised up a family of 8,000 youth cell group leaders for his church in Bogota, Columbia. His success began with a dream. His dream spurred him to pour his life into developing twelve multiplying cell leaders, who in turn have each raised up twelve multiplying cell leaders, and so on. He states, "The vision must take hold of your life, and you must be able to transmit that vision."[1]

Fajardo's success has eight simple, discernible elements:

1. He saw it. His dream was so vivid he could take a picture of it.
2. He saw it big. He saw an 18,000-seat auditorium full of students seeking God.
3. He saw it through the eyes of faith. He only had thirty kids, yet by faith he believed God would one day multiply thirty into a stadium full of young people.
4. He saw himself in the picture. He believed God could use him to make it happen.
5. He started where he was. He began to train the twelve he had in order to get to the 18,000 he didn't have.
6. He diligently poured his life into raising up other leaders. The focus of his time, energy, and effort for the next dozen years was training his twelve to multiply multipliers.
7. He kept focused on the dream over a long period of time. He stayed with it for twelve years until the dream became a reality.
8. God brought great results. Today the stadium is full on Saturday nights.

Changing the World by Raising Up Leaders

In 1931 a young man decided to spend two hours every morning in prayer before going to work. He continued for forty days. He took a map with him as he lay on his face before God in prayer in the Sierra Nevada Mountains. By the end of the forty days, he was seeing himself multiplying Christian leaders in every state in the United States and every continent. After the forty days of prayer, he began to turn his dream into reality by "training trainers of men."[2]

His commitment to multiplication of leaders was so effective that, by the beginning of World War II, Dawson Trotman and his resulting organization, The Navigators, had raised up "key men" for every ship in the United States Navy. He stated, "It thrills me to touch the life of a man who will touch a great host of men. Our best investment is with faithful men who shall be able to teach others also."[3]

He believed the multiplication of leaders was the key to "reaching the greatest number of people in the most effective way in the shortest possible time."[4] His method and his message was simply, "Produce reproducers."[5]

Dawson Trotman, died the way he lived—saving others. At the age of fifty, he went to be with the Lord after rescuing a non-swimmer from a cold lake. At his funeral Billy Graham said, "I think he touched more lives than any man I have ever known. We today represent thousands of people touched by this great man."[6]

Graham continued, "Dawson was a man of vision. When our God is small, the world looks big; but when our God is big, the world looks small. And Dawson saw the world as conquerable for Christ. To Dawson, God was big and the world was little. The day he went to be with the Lord some of his men arrived from Africa. One of his great visions was to open Africa. He was always dreaming, planning and scheming about new ways and means for reaching people for Christ."[7]

Trotman started in prayer. During his forty days of prayer, he began to pray over a map. God gave him the dream of multiplying leaders into every state and continent. For twenty-five years he kept his dream before him. After hard work and prayer in cooperation with God, the dream became a reality. His organization has continued on decades after he has been gone. One man, with one dream, made one big difference.

Dreaming Your Way to Success

The largest church in the world began as a dream. As he prayed over his church, God led the poor pastor to dream of seeing his tiny church grow to 150 members.

He has said, "At the time I had the capacity for believing for 150 members. I thought at the time that I would be eternally satisfied with that many people in my church. So I set a very clear goal of 150 members, and I wrote it down on a piece of paper and put it up on my wall. I also wrote the number on other slips of paper and put them everywhere, including my wallet. Everywhere I turned I saw the number 150. Eventually I was saturated with it."

"I began to eat with 150. I slept with the number 150 in my dreams. I was living with 150 members in my heart although I still did not have more than a few actual members in my congregation. After a while I began to preach as though I were speaking to 150 people, and I walked like a pastor who had 150 members.

"Before the first year was over, I had those 150 members! … When I had a clear-cut goal and began really to believe, then God answered my prayers and brought 150 members."[8]

He summarizes his story this way: "I was in a dilapidated tent church, but God said, "Dream." When I began to dream that the church was packed with people, people began to pour into the church … Keep on dreaming. You are going to grow only as big as your dream."[9]

As he prayed, God continued to lead him to dream. David Yonggi Cho later dreamed of 300 members, then 600 members, and saw God make it a reality. This has been the pattern of his faith-filled ministry as he eventually dreamed of 500,000 members with 50,000 cell groups and got it. His ability to hear God, dream big dreams, set clear goals, believe God for the goals, and structure his church to reach the goals, have made him the pastor of the largest church in the world.

His biographer has entitled his life story, *Dream Your Way to Success*. What's most exciting is that thousands of spiritual leaders have been raised up as a result of Cho listening to God, dreaming big and working hard to develop spiritual shepherds for his growing flock.

Watch Out!

You may not be used of God to raise up thousands of leaders, but you can be used of God to raise up several other multiplying spiritual leaders. That would be awesome by itself! And once the principle of multiplication kicks in, results could be astounding.

Scott, the pizza shop guy, worked for ten years to raise up four leaders. What if, in their lifetime, each of those four leaders multiplied four leaders of their own? And each of their four leaders multiplied four more leaders, and so on. After a few generations of multiplication, the results would be impressive.

The first generation of leaders	4 leaders
The second generation of leaders	4 X 4 = 16 leaders
The third generation of leaders	16 X 4 = 64 leaders
The fourth generation of leaders	64 X 4 = 256 leaders

The encouraging truth is that the vision of multiplying leaders is a possible dream. I began eighteen years ago with four potential leaders. After much prayer, learning from mistakes, hard work, and "divine luck," today our church has 125 small group leaders for adults and teens, from which we've planted three other new churches, which also have many leaders. The hardest part has been staying focused on the dream and keeping the dream alive.

You Gotta Have the Dream

Church researcher and best-selling author George Barna is blunt about the need for a dream. "Let's get one thing straight from the start. If you want to be a leader, vision is not an option; it is part of the standard equipment of a real leader ... "[10] He continues, "The equation is quite simple, no vision = no leadership."[11]

No one has ever become a multiplying leader without dreaming about it. You have to be like Scott, the pizza guy. You have to begin to dream of raising up at least one other leader.

Mountain-Moving Dreams

God-given dreams that are born from faith can accomplish seemingly impossible things. God gave Noah a detailed description of the ark so he could 'see it.' Because he could dream it, Noah was able to build it. Abram's name—meaning 'father'—gave him the dream of parenthood. God changed Abram's name to Abraham—'father of many'—to give him the dream of fathering many nations. And it became a reality. Joseph had the dream of being a great leader many years before it became a reality.

Jesus taught the need for mountain-moving dreams and faith when He said:

> Have faith in God, Jesus answered. I tell you the truth, if anyone says to this mountain, 'Go, throw yourself into the sea,' and does not doubt in his heart but believes that what he says will happen, it will be done for him. Therefore I tell you, whatever you ask for in prayer, believe that you have received it, and it will be yours.— Mark 11:22-24

> If you have faith as small as a mustard seed, you can say to this mulberry tree, 'Be uprooted and planted in the sea,' and it will obey you.—Luke 17:6

> I tell you the truth, if you have faith and do not doubt, not only can you do what was done to the fig tree, but also you can say to this mountain, 'Go, throw yourself into the sea,' and it will be done. If you believe, you will receive whatever you ask for in prayer.—Matthew 21:21-22

According to these three passages, it's not the size of our faith (*as small as a mustard seed*) but the object of our faith (Have faith in God) and the size of our dream (*this mountain*) that makes the difference. We have to believe and ask in prayer.

The writer of Hebrews reminds us that:

> And without faith it is impossible to please God, because anyone who comes to him must believe that he exists and that he rewards those who earnestly seek him. —Hebrews 11:6

Maybe you've been reluctant to believe God could or would use you to accomplish great things for Him. Let me encourage you that you're on solid biblical ground when you attempt great things for God and expect great things from God.

I want to encourage you to dream of God using you to multiply leaders. See yourself multiplying multipliers. It's a worthy dream. It's a powerful dream. It's a biblical dream.

Dream of Multiplying Leaders

Multiplying leaders is a biblical dream.

Multiplying leaders was both the strategy and the command of Jesus (Matthew 28:19-20). Robert Coleman, best-selling author of *The Master Plan of Evangelism* has stated, "Jesus came to save the world, and to that end He died, but on His way to the cross He concentrated His life on making a few disciples. These men were taught to do the same until through the process of reproduction, the gospel of the kingdom would reach to the ends of the earth."

Multiplying leaders was also the strategy and command of the apostle Paul as seen in the following verse:

And the things you have heard me say in the presence of many witnesses entrust to reliable men who will also be qualified to teach others. —2 Timothy 2:2

Notice that Timothy is commanded to reproduce what Paul had taught him into the lives of faithful men, who would be able to reproduce it into the lives of others.

Multiplying leaders is the fastest way to fulfill the great commission.

Leroy Eims shares an experience about how he discovered the power of multiplication: "Some time ago there was a display at the Museum of Science and Industry in Chicago. It featured a checkerboard with 1 grain of wheat on the first square, 2 on the second, 4 on the third, then 8, 16, 32, 64, 128, etc. Somewhere down the board, there were so many grains of wheat on the square that some were spilling over into neighboring squares—so here the demonstration stopped. Above the checkerboard display was a question, 'At this rate of doubling every square, how much grain would be on the checkerboards by the 64th square?'

"To find the answer to this riddle, you punched a button on the console in front of you, and the answer flashed on a little screen above the board: 'Enough to cover the entire subcontinent of India 50 feet deep.'[12]

"Multiplication may be costly, and in the initial stages, much slower than addition, but in the long run, it is the most effective way of accomplishing Christ's Great Commission ... and the only way."[13]

The *slow* process of raising up multiplying leaders is the *fastest* way to fulfill the Great Commission. The world is growing by multiplication and the church is growing through addition. In order to catch up with and keep pace with the multiplying population of the world, we must multiply multipliers.

Gene Warr, a successful businessman, explained his passion for raising up multiplying leaders by saying, "Time is too short to be putting in strokes where they do not count. How about you?"[14]

I like the way Waylon Moore puts it, "When the church exhales disciples it inhales converts."[15] He also states, "Disciple making has no prestige rating, no denominational category; but the results are consistently better than anything I have experienced in thirty years of working with people."[16]

Multiplying leaders leaves long term results.

Everyone wants to leave a legacy. We all want to be remembered fondly after we're gone. Multiplying leaders is a great way to have an impact that reaches long after we're off the scene.

Jesus left his disciples when he ascended into heaven. Yet the ministry of Jesus has grown and multiplied many times over because they were multiplying leaders. It has been noted, "you can begin spiritually multiplying yourself today, and start a dynamic process which could reach beyond your generation and into the next century."[17]

Multiplying leaders has practically unlimited potential.

Multiplying leaders is a seemingly small, slow, unappreciated process. But what is exciting to us 'ordinary' people is that by using this small process of multiplication we have a big impact. By using the slow process of multiplying leaders, we can reach the most people in the least amount of time. By practicing the principles of multiplying leaders, we can make an impact that thrills the heart of Jesus. We must remember that, "We need never fear beginning something quietly and on a small scale. God will cause what is his to grow."[18]

I like the fact that through multiplication I can have an impact in many places at the same time. In a sense my ministry extends far beyond my small group. At this church, my original group has multiplied to more than 125 groups, so my ministry can be in 125 places at once. I also have an influence on people who now lead ministries far beyond my geographic area. One of my "disciples" now oversees 500 group leaders at a Christian university. Others pastor churches in Chicago, Philadelphia, and New York City. One oversees hundreds of missionaries. So in a sense, multiplying disciple-makers can touch the world through the leaders they develop.

Eight Essentials for Going from Dream to Reality

From the above-mentioned Scriptures, and from the examples of small group leaders who have raised up spiritual leaders, there seem to be eight essentials for going from dream to reality.

1. Get with God and get His dream for your life and ministry.
2. Write it down and picture it.
3. Refer to it frequently.
4. Believe God can and will do it.
5. Ask God to do it.
6. Plan to fulfill your part.
7. Work like it all depends on you. Pray like it all depends on God.
8. Start small, but speak and live like the dream is becoming a reality.

You probably aren't ready to dream of a church with 500,000 members. But if you're an effective small group leader, there's no reason you shouldn't be dreaming of cooperating with God in raising at least one other healthy, growing, effective, multiplying spiritual leader. It all starts with the dream.

I believe you must already have a dream to cooperate with God in raising up growing, healthy, multiplying leaders who will make a difference. This book will help you get there. There are eight essentials for mentoring multiplying leaders. The first is to dream.

The Small Group Leader's Dream of Mentoring Healthy, Growing, Maturing Leaders

- Get with God and get His dream for your life and ministry.

- Write it down and picture it. Feel free to use one of these statements that may apply:

  - I have a dream of mentoring one other healthy, growing, multiplying leader.

  - I believe God would use me to raise up an army of small group leaders.

  - I believe God wants me to focus on developing five multiplying leaders the next couple of years.

- Sign and date this dream.

- Refer to it frequently. Read it regularly and make it an ongoing focus for prayer, learning, and effort.

- Believe God can and will do it.

- Make it a daily prayer request until the dream has become a reality.

- Plan to fulfill your part. If you're already mentoring a leader or leaders, plan what you need to do to help them multiply as leaders.

- Work like it all depends on you. Pray like it all depends on God.

- Speak and live like the dream is becoming a reality.

DEMONSTRATE:

Demonstrate Multiplying Leadership

Show Me How

I committed my life to God halfway through high school. Not long after that, I came in contact with some materials that showed me how to pray 30 minutes a day and how to study the Bible devotionally. By following them, I learned how to have a vibrant daily quiet time.

Right out of high school, I spent a summer on a mission trip to England with 30-40 other kids. Part of our daily schedule was to have a quiet time. After a few weeks, one of the other guys came up to me and said, "You seem to be the only one who really gets much from having a quiet time. Would you show me how you do it?"

The next day he and I had quiet time together and I began to show him what to do. Word of what we were doing leaked out. Soon half a dozen guys were having quiet time with me daily. It wasn't always 'quiet' but they did learn to meet with God. And I learned the power of demonstration.

I Want That

When I went off to a Christian college, I continued my vibrant quiet time practices. I also began to pray that God would give me someone into whom I could reproduce my life. After two weeks of prayer, a fellow student named Darrell approached me. "I heard about your times with God. I want that. Could you show me how you do it?"

Here was a Christian college sophomore who desperately wanted to spend meaningful times with God, yet wasn't sure how. He didn't need more motivation, inspiration, or condemnation. He needed demonstration. We began to meet daily. Later he wanted me to show him how to do evangelism and how to go on a Christian date. (I found the last one to be fun to demonstrate).

I'm convinced there are hungry-hearted people all around us. They don't need more motivation, inspiration, or condemnation. They need demonstration, leading to transformation. There are people who *will* get saved, if we'll just show them how. There are people who *will* have quiet time, if we'll but show them how. There are people who *will* do evangelism and follow-up, if we'll train them to do it. And there are people who *will* become multiplying leaders, if we'll apply the power of demonstration. Effective demonstration centers on two things: modeling the right methods and showing others how to do them. Both are needed.

> The second step for developing new small group leaders is demonstrating multiplying leadership for them.

Model Effective Leadership

Highly influential medical missionary Albert Schweitzer observed, "Example is not the main thing influencing others. It is the only thing."[1] Those who effectively multiply their ministry start by modeling multiplying ministry. You have to produce before you can reproduce. Experience proves that leadership and multiplication are more often caught than taught.

The best-selling Christian leadership author John Maxwell has frequently said, "It takes a leader to make a leader." Robert Coleman raises the banner of example when he says, "One living sermon is worth one hundred explanations."[2] Waylon Moore wisely concludes, "Since it takes a disciple to build other disciples, the chain of multiplication begins with you."[3]

You have to model the type of leadership you want to develop in others. There are two aspects of modeling multiplying leadership that are especially important. These include: the seven character requirements for multiplied ministry and the eight habits of the effective small group leader.

Model the Seven Character Requirements for Multiplied Ministry

The Bible describes seven character requirements for greater fruitfulness and multiplied harvest. Interestingly these biblical requirements for multiplied ministry are the same characteristics found in transformational, multiplying leaders.

1. Sacrifice

> I tell you the truth, unless a kernel of wheat falls to the ground and dies, it remains only a single seed. But if it dies, it produces many seeds. —John 12:24

In this passage, Jesus tells us that death was the secret of a single kernel being multiplied into many. The principle is that there is no multiplication without sacrifice. Sacrifice is the foundational characteristic of multiplying leaders.

Multiplying leaders set the pace in terms of commitment. Some of the best multipliers in the world are at ICM in Bogota, Columbia—a church that exploded to 16,000 cells in a twelve-year period. An analysis of these leaders states, "One secret of ICM's success is the high level commitment of the leadership. ICMers are sold out to the Lord's work, and their time commitment reflects that fact."[4]

Every fruitful small group leader practices sacrifice. Multiplying leaders know they must 'die' to many good things in order to accomplish the best things. They're willing to 'die' to spending their lives following selfish pursuits in order to achieve kingdom business and multiplied results. They know it's the time spent outside the group meeting—time spent praying, inviting, contacting, and mentoring—that makes the difference in group growth and multiplication.

Martin Luther King stated, "If a man hasn't discovered what he will die for, he is not fit to live."[5] The truth is this, if you're not ready to sacrifice, you will not multiply.

Randall Neighbour, President of TOUCH Outreach Ministries writes, "[Small group leadership] is earned through servanthood and prayer. When you love people by laying down your life for each of them and love them just where they are in life, they will respect you and follow you."[6]

Another element of dying that is essential for multiplying is getting out of the way. Some of us enjoy ministry so much we don't know how to get out the way to let others have their chance. This attitude blocks multiplication. We have to 'die' to our need to be needed and get over our insecurities if we ever hope to raise up multiplying leaders.

2. Dependence on God

This is what the LORD says: "Cursed is the one who trusts in man, who depends on flesh for his strength and whose heart turns away from the LORD. He will be like a bush in the wastelands; he will not see prosperity when it comes. He will dwell in the parched places of the desert, in a salt land where no one lives. But blessed is the man who trusts in the LORD, whose confidence is in him. He will be like a tree planted by the water that sends out its roots by the stream. It does not fear when heat comes; its leaves are always green. It has no worries in a year of drought and never fails to bear fruit." —Jeremiah 17:5-8

The Lord told Jeremiah that depending solely on human resources would lead to barrenness. But depending upon the Lord would yield a lifestyle of fruitfulness.

Multiplying leaders is a God-sized task requiring dependence on God for success. In our strength, we can't save anyone's soul. We can't transform the lives of others and set them free. We can't make them effective multiplying leaders. But God can. And He will, if we trust Him.

I like the way Randall Neighbour describes the size of our task and the need for dependence in fruitful ministry:

"From a human perspective, it does look like a mountain of responsibility to move with a spoon, doesn't it? But that's not reality. If you are called of God to be a cell leader, you will be drawing from an energy source much greater than yourself. It is miraculous how God works through us when we are working within our calling and at the pace He desires for us."[7]

Dependence is expressed by prayer. I ask my high school leaders to spend at least five minutes each day praying especially for our group. Some pray more. But I'm happy if they at least hit the five minutes each day.

David Yonggi Cho, pastor of the largest church in the world and the spiritual 'father' of tens of thousands of cell leaders, has said, "The most important thing in our lives is prayer."[8] His dependence upon God is clear when he says, "I am not able to do all I have been called to do without spending the minimum of one hour a day in prayer every morning."[9]

In speaking of the power of his example in prayer, he writes, "At the Yoido Full Gospel Church in Seoul, we teach our new converts about prayer. Yet, if I did not pray, they would not pray."[10] His dependence upon God in prayer is obvious when he states, "One of the greatest lies of Satan is that we just don't have time to pray. However, all of us have enough time to sleep, eat, and breathe. As soon as we realize that prayer is as important as sleeping, eating and breathing, we will be amazed at how much more time will be available to us to pray."[11]

3. Intimate Connection with Jesus

> Remain in me, and I will remain in you. No branch can bear fruit by itself; it must remain in the vine. Neither can you bear fruit unless you remain in me. I am the vine; you are the branches. If a man remains in me and I in him, he will bear much fruit; apart from me you can do nothing. —John 15:4-5

Jesus is the fruit maker. In order to bear fruit we must be so intimately connected to Him that He actually bears the fruit through us. Otherwise we will accomplish nothing.

There are many ingredients for an intimate relationship. These include honesty, openness, communication, sharing, trust, conflict resolution, shared experiences, acceptance, availability, and time. Yet the most important might be time, because the others would not occur without it. In order to be fruitfully connected to God, we must spend time with God.

I generally spend about half an hour to forty-five minutes in the Word and prayer each morning. I also try to spend a couple of hours one morning a week primarily in prayer. Some of our leaders like to listen to the Bible on tape and pray when they commute to and from work each day. Some try to spend time each evening in the Word and prayer. Multiplying leaders take the time to stay intimately connected to Jesus in the Word and prayer.

I find it challenging to hear of the amount of time others may spend in personal devotions. In researching cell leaders in some of the world's largest cell churches, Joel Comiskey found that, "Those who spend 90 minutes or more in devotions per day multiply their groups twice as much as those who spend less than 30 minutes."[12] Those who multiply leaders take the time to stay intimately connected to Jesus in the Word and prayer.

4. Persevering Labor and Hard Work

> Let us not become weary in doing good, for at the proper time we will reap a harvest if we do not give up. —Galatians 6:9

The harvest follows hard work. Multiplying leaders is the result of diligent labor. Comiskey's research confirms this biblical principle. He writes, "I discovered that the potential to lead a healthy, successful cell group does not reside with the gifted, the educated, or those with vibrant personalities. The answer rather is hard work."[13]

Andrew Carnegie moved to America as a boy and soon began working in a cotton mill. He later moved on to the telegraph office of the railroad. He kept working and eventually built the mammoth Carnegie Steel Company. He became one of the richest men in America and used his fortune to establish many scientific, educational, and cultural institutions. His company sponsored the creation of thousands of libraries throughout the world. He summarized the secret of his success with these words: "The average person puts in only 25 percent of his energy and ability into his work. The world takes off its hat to those who put in more than 50 percent of their capacity, and stands on its head for those few and far between souls who devote 100 percent."[14]

Multiplying leaders comes from working hard and doing good over and over and over again, even when you're too tired, too busy and don't feel like it anymore. Too often leaders start out enthusiastically down the path of multiplication. But they give up too soon. We must not grow weary in the hard work of doing good if we want to reap a harvest.

5. Patient Effort

> Be patient, then, brothers, until the Lord's coming. See how the farmer waits for the land to yield its valuable crop and how patient he is for the autumn and spring rains. —James 5:7

Farmers have to be patient. They plow the soil, plant the seed, fertilize it, water it, weed it, and wait. They have to wait for the seed to mature and yield a harvest. Great harvests don't come overnight. They take time. The principle is clear: great fruitfulness comes through great patience.

Claude and Ginny started a group for single adults in our church. The first night they had only one other person come. But they kept patiently plowing ahead. They dreamed. They invited. They prayed. Slowly the group began to grow. In just a couple of years they've multiplied into ten table groups that gather after a worship service of sixty-five single adults every Tuesday night.

It took Brian and Susie almost a year of patient effort until their group began to grow, and nearly another year before it multiplied. Multiplying leaders take time and patience. You have to keep on praying, keep on dreaming, and keep on investing. Yet the results are worth the time and effort. The slow, painful process of the true spiritual multiplication of leaders is the fastest way to reach the most people.

6. Saturation with the Word of God

> Blessed is the man who does not walk in the counsel of the wicked or stand in the way of sinners or sit in the seat of mockers. But his delight is in the law of the LORD, and on his law he meditates day and night. He is like a tree planted by streams of water, which yields its fruit in season and whose leaf does not wither. Whatever he does prospers. —Psalms 1:1-3

Psalms promises steady fruitfulness to those who practice saturation in the Word of God. Delight in the Word of God and the God of the Word will give you a life of stability (a tree planted), productivity (yields its fruit), durability (leaf does not wither), and prosperity (whatever he does will prosper).

7. Focused Vision on the Harvest

> Do you not say, 'Four months more and then the harvest'? I tell you, open your eyes and look at the fields! They are ripe for harvest. —John 4:35

In John 4:35, Jesus is telling his disciples that in order to reap a harvest they have to "open up their eyes and look at" it. Farmers have to 'see' a harvest even when it's just an empty field. Leaders who multiply leaders have spiritual vision to 'see' opportunities where others see obstacles. They 'see' future leaders where others do not. They 'picture' potential and possibilities when others see hindrances and hopelessness.

George Barna describes this necessary spiritual ability to 'see' with these words, "Vision is a picture held in your mind's eye of the way things could or should be in the days ahead. Vision connotes a visual reality, a portrait of conditions that do not exist currently. This picture is internalized and personal."[15]

Model the Eight Habits of Effective Small Group Leader

There are eight habits practiced by the leaders of small groups that grow and multiply. In twenty-six years of leading groups and group leaders, I've found there are eight habits practiced by the leaders of healthy, growing multiplying groups. When practiced, these habits work and groups grow and multiply. When neglected, groups fail to sustain growth to multiplication.

A detailed and highly practical description of each of these habits is found in the book, *The Eight Habits of Effective Small Group Leaders*, (TOUCH Outreach Ministries, 2001,) These habits were confirmed when Joel Comiskey surveyed 700 effective small group leaders from around the world. He found they had these eight common denominators.[16] Before you can multiply healthy, growing, multiplying small groups, you need to lead or have led such groups by applying these habits. A summary of these eight habits follows:

1. Dream. Write out specific goals for the growth and multiplication of the group you lead.
2. Pray for your group members and multiplication daily.
3. Invite new people to your group weekly.
4. Contact group members regularly.
5. Prepare for your group meeting.
6. Have and mentor apprentice leaders.
7. Plan group fellowship activities.
8. Be committed to personal growth.

Multiply Leaders by Showing Them How

When my youngest son was seven, he was on a baseball team that was an exercise in futility. Although the team had a nice coach and plenty of athletic kids, it always lost. The kids just couldn't hit, throw, or catch the ball. I hated to go to the games because I hated seeing the frustration in the kids' faces.

At the end of the year banquet, the coach announced that he wasn't going to coach the next year and asked if anyone would be interested. I had successfully coached my older boys and had confidence that, with some demonstration, that team would win. My wife nudged me and I volunteered. I was so confident in the power of demonstration I even announced that we'd finish in the top four of the league the next year.

At the beginning of the next season, I made it my goal to tell them *what*, tell them *why* and *show them how* to hit, throw, field, and run the bases. We broke each of the large skills—throwing, fielding, hitting, and base running—into a series of smaller skills, and practiced them over and over. For example, to throw, we showed them how to turn their opposite shoulder, step toward the person they were throwing to, and throw, with their throwing hand pointing toward the glove for which they were aiming. Soon they were throwing with greater strength, distance, and accuracy. As a result, their confidence greatly improved.

The same kids who had lost almost every game the year before won the first seven games in a row. Then we hit a spell where the kids 'forgot' how to do it and got sloppy. So we lost a few games heading into the end-of-season tournament. This caused their teachability to return.

Before the tournament, we held a couple of practices to go over the fundamentals of throwing, fielding, base running, and hitting. The power of demonstration took over. We got hot, won six of seven games and made it to the finals in a league of fourteen teams. We had to play the team everyone feared. They hadn't lost a game in several years.

The day before the game, we had another practice. After reviewing the fundamentals, their confidence was high. They believed they could win. The next night they easily defeated the previously undefeated team. Never underestimate the power of demonstration!

Too often good people get discouraged in living the Christian life, simply because no one has ever shown them how. They think they can't pray or witness or lead a group, just because they haven't been shown how it's done.

In order to multiply leaders, you must use the power of demonstration. You must be committed to telling them what you're doing, why you're doing it, and how to do it most effectively.

Intentional Demonstration

Recently I began training a handful of ninth-grade guys and several adults to become multiplying small group leaders. I was overly intentional about demonstrating every aspect of leading this group. We were taking our time and 'doing it right.' We went over each of the eight habits in detail and I carefully demonstrated every aspect of effective group leadership, from how to dream, to prayer and fasting, to inviting people to the group, to meaningful contacting of group members.

I showed them how to prepare for the group meeting, how to mentor apprentices, how to plan group social activities, and how to set up a personal growth plan. And the good news is, they got it! As a result they had confidence that God would use them as effective leaders because "they know how." This group successfully multiplied in less than a year.

God can use you to multiply leaders. But you have to use the power of demonstration. You have to model the habits and characteristics, and you must show them how to do the skills.

The Multiplying Leader's Demonstration Worksheet

- When it comes to modeling leadership, which of the seven character requirements (sacrifice, dependence on God, connected to Christ, etc.) is easiest for you to live?

  Which is most difficult?

- Which of the eight habits of an effective leader is easiest for you to do?

  Which is most difficult?

- Which tasks of effective demonstration come most naturally to you?

  Which is most difficult?

- What is a skill of leadership you can demonstrate for your potential leader this week?

DISCOVER:

Discover Potential Leaders

You Can't Have Babies if You Don't Get Pregnant

The third step for developing new small group leaders is to be on the lookout to discover potential leaders.

Our church has more than 125 small groups for adults and teens. Some of our leaders have multiplied themselves and their group several times. There are a few that have existed for years without multiplying. The multipliers are always on the lookout for potential leaders and always have several apprentices. The non-multipliers struggle to be able to get or keep an apprentice.

We desire that no leaders in our church start a new group unless, and until, they each have an apprentice who's being mentored to launch his or her own group. The reason: if you don't discover and develop potential leaders, you will not multiply leaders. It's great to lead highly 'pregnant' groups with several apprentices. These groups can always multiply.

35

Who to Look For

Start by considering everyone as a potential candidate for small group leadership. Bill Donahue and Russ Robinson suggest that, "Rather than looking for leaders, we suggest that you look for people. There's always a greater supply of people than obvious leaders."[1]

God uses unlikely and ordinary people. The founder of the Hebrew nation, Abraham, was a herdsman. Israel's best king, David, had been a shepherd boy. The disciples were such unlikely sorts as uneducated Galilean fishermen and tax collectors.

I'm glad God is big enough to use foolish, weak, lowly people (like me) to reveal His glory and power. That's one reason I love 1 Corinthians 1:26-29 so much. It says,

> Brothers, think of what you were when you were called. Not many of you were wise by human standards; not many were influential; not many were of noble birth. But God chose the foolish things of the world to shame the wise; God chose the weak things of the world to shame the strong. He chose the lowly things of this world and the despised things—and the things that are not—to nullify the things that are, so that no one may boast before him.
> —1 Corinthians 1:26-29

Everyone Can Lead a Small Group

The Bible clearly teaches that ministry is not reserved for the ordained clergy. All of God's people are to be trained to do the work of the ministry. Every member is to be a minister. Therefore, every member can be trained for leadership.

> It was he who gave some to be apostles, some to be prophets, some to be evangelists, and some to be pastors and teachers, to prepare God's people for works of service, so that the body of Christ may be built up.—Ephesians 4:11-12

The Bible also teaches that every believer is to be a disciple. And to truly be a disciple you must be a disciple-maker. Therefore, every member should be discipled to disciple others.

Therefore go and make disciples of all nations, baptizing them in the name of the Father and of the Son and of the Holy Spirit, and teaching them to obey everything I have commanded you. And surely I am with you always, to the very end of the age.
—Matthew 28:19-20

Experience shows that leadership development and discipleship happen best in the small group ministry of a local church. The churches experiencing explosive and healthy growth are the churches that are raising up disciple-making leaders in their small groups to lead their small groups. And they do it with the philosophy that anyone can become a cell group leader. One pastor states, "We do not speak of 'cell members' any longer, but of trainees to become cell leaders."[2] Another says, "Training [for cell leadership] is not optional."[3]

Everyone can lead a small group. Don't overlook anyone or take the potential of anyone lightly.

Where to Look

Look in your current group.

This is the most obvious place to look for potential leaders. These are people with whom you already have a relationship. They already know the other people in the group. They've observed how God has used you to lead the group.

Look in past groups.

Maybe there are some people who were a part of your group in the past but currently are not. Maybe they got out of groups for a season. Maybe they moved in a different direction through group multiplication. Maybe they became group leaders under someone else, but are out from that sphere at this time. These are people you already have a relationship with, who may now be ready to serve as great leadership apprentices.

Look around your church.

There are probably people who attend worship services faithfully but, for whatever reason, have failed to get in a group or are no longer in a group. Look around on Sundays for such people. Invite them to your group and see where it goes from there.

Look in your family.

Sometimes our best ministry is in our own home. The New Testament leaders James and Jude were both half-brothers of Jesus Christ. Currently, some of my top trainees are my elder sons.

Look at friends.

When looking for potential leaders, look at your friends and your friends' friends. Also look at the friends of your children and their parents. The parents of our children have become some of our most fruitful relationships.

Look at new converts.

New Christians can make great apprentices for several reasons. They have more contacts with non-Christians and are often evangelistic. They're enthusiastic. They're teachable. And they can be highly contagious spiritually.

Look where you might not think to look.

Bill Donahue tells of a quiet, shy, unlikely man in his group named Stan. By default, Stan ended up leading the group one day. He said, "[Stan] shocked us. After preparing for three hours, he led a veritable clinic on how to lead a small group. His questions were probing, his feedback encouraging, and his insight into people's lives profound. He guided us through a lively discussion that had both depth and a call to action … It was the best group we'd had in months … I would not have chosen Stan. But God saw something in Stan that I could not. When given the opportunity to lead in the context of safe relationships, Stan rose to the occasion."[4]

Everyone Can Lead a Small Group But Some People Will Multiply Faster than Others

Effective discipleship, mentoring, and leadership training will take a significant commitment from you. You want your efforts to be as fruitful as possible. This desire for optimal fruitfulness calls for wise selectivity. You want to invest in the people who will go the furthest the fastest.

Jesus didn't select everyone to be His disciples. He carefully selected twelve and passed up some others. There are seasons when we can't be very selective when it comes to seeking potential leaders. But there is often great value in being selective.

Jim Collins, in his book *Good to Great*, details the characteristics of the rare corporations that have made the jump from run-of-the-mill companies to greatness and sustained it. One of the common characteristics is what Collins calls the ability "to get the right people on the bus."[5] Getting the right people on the bus will require less managing and motivating from the leader.

When it comes to selecting potential leaders in whom you'll heavily invest your life, it's wise 'to get the right people on your leadership bus.' John Maxwell writes, "You must select the right people for your organization. If you select well, the benefits are multiplied and seem nearly endless. If you select poorly, the problems are multiplied and seem endless."[6]

While anyone with the right motivation and training can lead a group, not everyone seems to be able to multiply group leaders. Learn to look for "the right people" to get on your leadership training bus.

The higher the level of leadership, the more careful we should be in the selection process. For example, as a pastor I'm much more selective in choosing paid staff than volunteer group apprentices.

Qualities to Look For

There are various lists of qualities to look for in potential leaders. For example, Paul told Timothy the quality to seek was faithfulness (2 Timothy 2:2). Some like to expand that a little and look for F.A.T. people. (Relax, it's an acrostic for Faithful, Available, and Teachable).

Paul Yonggi Cho looks for five qualities: enthusiasm, testimony, dedication, spirit-filled, and availability because of adequate time and money.[7] John Maxwell gives ten qualities for potential leaders: character, influence, positive attitude, excellent people skills, evident gifts, proven track record, confidence, self-discipline, effective communication skills, and discontentment with the status quo.[8] And, of course, God looks at the heart (1 Samuel 16:7), wanting it to be fully committed to Him (2 Chronicles 16:9).

I recommend you make your own list of those qualities you deem most important in your setting. You may want to compare and get input from your coach, pastor, or other small group leaders in your church. Realize that the fewer qualities on the list, the more people will qualify. Likewise, the more qualities on your list, the fewer people will qualify.

The following are some of the practical considerations in selecting a potential leader to mentor:

A philosophy of life similar to yours

A person's values and priorities need to mesh with your own. Otherwise both of you will get frustrated. "If you don't have the basics in common, you may end up working at cross-purposes, and you won't experience the effectiveness you would like."[9]

A potential in which you strongly believe

You won't put out the full effort necessary unless you strongly believe in the potential of your prospective leaders. If you have serious doubts about their potential, give them a few tests. See how they do on them. If they disappoint you, keep looking.

A personality you're best suited to impact

We all have different personalities. I'm intense. One of our other pastors, Rod, is more laid back. Some people respond to him better than to me and vice versa. I'm a strong leader. Steve, another pastor at our church, is a patient pastor. Some people connect with his style better than mine. Others respond better to me.

If a person has potential but perhaps isn't a good fit with your personality, work with your coach or another small group leader to get that person under the right mentor.

How to Look

Look prayerfully.

God is always looking for potential leaders. He wants to strengthen those with hearts fully committed to Him. He wants to use some to stand in the gap on behalf of others.

Multiplying leaders means cooperating with God in *His* plan to find and mentor potential leaders into multiplying leaders. It's getting in on what God is already doing.

> The key to discovering potential leaders is praying persistent prayers.

It's working with God in discovering potential leaders. Therefore, prayer is of the utmost importance.

Jesus is our example in all things, including selecting potential leaders. Note that He practiced the principle of discovering leaders through prayer:

One of those days Jesus went out to a mountainside to pray, and spent the night praying to God. When morning came, he called his disciples to him and chose twelve of them, whom he also designated apostles.—Luke 6:12-13

Jesus not only practiced the principle of discovering leaders through prayer, He told us to do the same. Note what He told His disciples: "The harvest is plentiful but the workers are few. Ask the Lord of the harvest, therefore, to send out workers into his harvest field" (Matthew 9:37-38).

In my second year of college, I became fired up about spiritual reproduction. I wanted to reproduce, but I had no disciples. So I began to make it an important part of my prayer life. Daily I prayed, "Lord, give me a disciple." Exactly two weeks later a fellow student approached me about discipling him. The only time we were able to meet was after "lights out," and the only place available was in the dorm bathroom/shower area. So we began to meet every night and, jokingly, called ourselves the Bathroom Baptist Temple.

It was so fulfilling I began to ask God for another disciple. Exactly two weeks later, a guy approached us and said, "I've been brushing my teeth down the way every night the last two weeks. I'd really love to get in on what you're doing. Can I join?" So the Bathroom Baptist Temple expanded from two to three.

It was so much fun, I began to ask for another disciple. Exactly two weeks later another guy approached us. He was the roommate of the second guy. He said, "I don't know what you guys are doing every night, but my roommate is a different person. How do I join the Bathroom Baptist Temple?" So the B.B.T. went from three to four.

We had such a good time I began to ask for yet another disciple. Exactly two weeks later, we added our fifth member. He also had seen what we were doing and wanted to be a part. At this point the dorm supervisor gave us our own meeting room.

It was one of the best times of my life. I had the opportunity to pour my life into some young men. We developed good friendships. All of us grew from the accountability of the group. They said the group changed their lives. The next semester our group multiplied into five groups, with each of the original members as a leader. And I learned that the key for discovering potential leaders was persistent prayer.

Look patiently.

It will probably take more than two weeks of prayer to discover the potential leader(s) to be mentored for leadership. That can be a good thing. When possible, take some time to make sure. John Wimber, the founder of the Vineyard Association of Churches, is remembered for saying, "Select slow to grow fast." A few of the right people will go further faster than many of the wrong ones.

You'll invest hundreds of hours in training the potential leader to lead and to multiply leadership. Be a wise steward of your time, and be patient in the selection process. Also, let me suggest that once you've selected potential leaders, don't give them a title too soon. Before they have a title, you have more options available than after they have a title. "Giving a title is like skydiving: once you've jumped out of the plane, you're committed."[10]

Look wisely.

Wise selection not only accelerates the multiplication process, it also limits the *deceleration* process. It's possible to get the right person at the wrong time. Those who have a bad experience will be reluctant to try leadership in the future. Also, they may cause others to have a bad experience with groups and not be willing to get involved in the future.

What to Watch Out For

People with Overwhelming Life Situations

There is such a thing as the right person but the wrong time. Someone with an overwhelming life situation won't have the time needed to train effectively. Different people are overwhelmed by different situations, which may include such challenges as having a new baby, a serious illness suffered by them or a close family member, a teenager in rebellion, or a divorce. People in these situations may need the group at this time, but may not be ready to train to enter training.

People with Excessive Emotional Baggage

People with excessive emotional baggage probably won't have the stamina to go through the rigors, demands, and disappointments of leadership. In Mark chapter 5, Jesus cast a legion of demons from a man who had been living in a graveyard. The delighted man asked to go with Jesus. Yet Jesus told him to go home to tell his family and friends what God had done for him (Mark 5:19). When selecting people with excessive emotional baggage, be sure it's what God is leading you to do.

People with "Killer" Attitudes

There are certain individual attitudes God considers very dangerous to the health of the whole group. The Bible records several occasions when leaders with one of these attitudes were so out of line and dangerous that God killed them. People with these attitudes are very dangerous to place in leadership. Be very careful in selecting such people. These "killer" attitudes include:

- *Fear and grumbling.* In the book of Numbers, ten men spread the negative report about the Promised Land. God considered this to be so serious that they were killed by a plague. (Numbers 15)
- *Rebellion.* Korah and some friends stood up against Moses in bold rebellion. God considered such a deed to be so dangerous that the ground opened up to swallow Korah and his friends alive. Beyond that, God sent fire to burn up 250 of his followers because they rebelled against God's chosen leadership. (Exodus 16)
- *Dishonesty.* Ananias and Sapphira sold some land and gave part of the profits to God. Yet they lied and bragged that they were giving all of it. God regarded such a deed to be so dangerous that they died instantly. (Acts 5)
- *Arrogance.* Herod elevated himself and refused to give glory to God. God was not impressed and Herod was struck down and eaten by worms. (Acts 12)

These Bible stories remind us of the sobering seriousness of seeking God-hearted people for potential positions of leadership. They should help us focus on the importance of prayerful, and patient wisdom in selecting potential leaders.

Look persistently.

Leaders who effectively multiply their ministry are always on the lookout for potential leaders. They always have their eyes open for people with a spark of potential. Discovering potential leaders is not something that's done once and forgotten. It's a lifestyle.

I keep both a mental and written list of potential leaders. I regularly discuss potential leaders with leaders. I write names down on my prayer list and pray about certain people for certain roles.

Discovering potential leaders is an ongoing challenge. It's a never-ending job and a great joy. It can be very fulfilling and at times very frustrating. But it must be done. The next generation is the only hope for the future.

The Multiplying Leaders Discovery Worksheet

I am currently mentoring one or more potential leaders: True or False?

I'm on the lookout for possible leaders. True of False? If so, how may?

Places I haven't looked include:

The qualities I think are most important for the possible leaders I'm looking for include:

I will begin to pray seriously about the following possible people:

DEEPEN:

Deepen The Relationship

When I was a teenager my youth pastor was Lee Simmons. He poured his life into several young men, who eventually became pastors, including me. He had a dream of helping us mature in Christ and in ministry. He demonstrated to us a life of effective ministry. He selected a few people he believed had ministry potential (I think a few of us selected him more than he selected us). And he built a relationship with us. He played softball with us, taught us to water ski, and wrestled with us. We were at his house so much that it sometimes annoyed his wife. He influenced us because he built a relationship with us.

Jesus called twelve to be with Him (Mark 3:13). I don't think they played softball or went water skiing together, although Jesus and Peter did water walk, which is even more difficult! They did eat, walk, minister, and 'camp out' together often. He built an influential relationship with them. He later told them He loved them (John 15:9, 12). He called them his friends (John 15:15). Jesus developed His disciples, in part, by building a relationship with them.

Paul also mentored potential leaders by using the essential of a deepening relationship. He trained others the way Barnabas had trained him, by taking them along *with him* (Acts 9:27, 13:4, 13:13, 15:40, 16:3). While travelling they ate, walked, ministered, and worked *together*. In order to train Aquila and Priscilla, he lived with them and worked with them for a time (Acts 18:3). To train Apollos, the three of them invited him to stay with them (Acts 18:26). One reason Paul multiplied leaders was because he built a relationship with them.

A good football coach coaches players, not just football. A successful math teacher teaches students, not just math. An effective multiplier mentors leaders and doesn't merely communicate skills. There's no discipleship without relationship! The length and breadth of our influence on others is related to the depth of our relationship with them. After you've discovered potential leaders, you need to deepen your relationship with them.

> The fourth step for developing new small group leaders is deepening your relationship with them.

Our worship pastor is mentoring our associate worship pastor with great success. He doesn't always follow the other essentials of leadership development, but he always does this one. Don't underestimate the power and the importance of deepening relationships with your potential leaders.

It Begins With Caring

We all know that *people don't care how much you know until they know how much you care.* Developing a deepening relationship isn't overly complicated. It begins by simply caring for someone. Caring is giving people emotional food. Using CARE as an acrostic, we can see four components required for effective caring.

C: Communicate
People feel closer to you and more responsive to what you say when you take the time to communicate with them.

One small groups pastor I know makes the effort to be a good communicator with his leaders and they appreciate it. All of them receive an e-mail from him every week with a sermon series lesson and other pertinent information. He calls leaders on Saturday mornings. He eats breakfast with his coaches every few weeks and has had them in his home on several occasions.

A lack of communication is frustrating. I had a boss who was a great public communicator, but a poor one in private. He was extremely busy with many responsibilities. As a result, he didn't take the time to tell me what he expected or how I was doing, even though I tried to get some feedback. I worked very hard doing what I hoped he wanted done.

After several months of limited communication, he did something that was very difficult to handle. At a large staff meeting, he told everyone how disappointed he was that some things weren't getting done in my area of ministry. I was devastated. I had no idea he wanted those things done until that night. I learned the painful frustration of trying to please someone who wouldn't communicate.

People deserve to know what's going on. Take the time to communicate regularly with your potential leaders early and often. Call them. E-mail them. Write them. Visit them. Invite them over.

Share your expectations. Let them know how they're doing. Tell them what you've planned for the coming group meetings. Give them calendars, schedules, and goal sheets. Share with them how you feel things are going. Communicate!

A: Appreciate

In the 1930s, a young YMCA teacher taught a popular class on getting along with people. He taught what he called "the big secret in dealing with people." It was, " Be hearty in approbation [formal appreciation] and lavish in your praise." Dale Carnegie later wrote his ideas in what became one of the best-selling books in history, *How to Win Friends and Influence People*. It still sells well today.

People will go to great efforts when they feel appreciated. I've learned that people are *appreciating* assets when they are *appreciated* assets. As William James had noted, "The deepest principle in human nature is the desire to be appreciated."

Multiplying leaders can show appreciation for their potential leaders by giving them cards, books, tapes, magazine subscriptions, t-shirts, or gifts certificates. A few weeks ago our children's ministry coordinator gave her teachers candy 'life savers' stapled to a card telling them she appreciated them as 'life savers' in children's ministry.

R: Recognize

When my boys were little, they said three particular words more than any others. Do you know what they were? They'd climb up the slide and yell, "Look at me!" They'd hang upside down from the monkey bars and shout, "Daddy, look at me." Or they'd come out of my room wearing my 'big man' clothes on their 'little boy' bodies and scream in delight, "Daddy, look at me." People have a natural need to be recognized.

I try to have special times each year when I formally recognize my top staff in front of each other. In August we go out to eat and have a lot of laughs as I give them the annual coveted "Earley Award," recognizing their major contribution to our church in the previous year. Usually at the Christmas banquet, I mention each one by name and give them a gift.

I've also learned the value of trying to recognize them from the pulpit or in front of their peers at a staff meeting. They, of course, like to be recognized in private settings as well as public ones. We all need to learn to find out what others are doing well, and then recognize it.

E: Encourage

Encouragement is oxygen for the soul. When Rich DeVos, the multimillionaire founder of Amway, was asked which is the greatest management skill, he replied, "How to be a cheerleader."

The word *encouragement* speaks of coming alongside another and giving that person courage. Leadership is a fearful thing. Everyone needs someone drawing alongside, saying, "You can do it. Don't quit." We all need someone who believes in us. Everyone needs encouragement.

I was a very shy high school student. Yet, my youth pastor, Lee Simmons, kept encouraging and pushing me to get out of my comfort zone and minister. He 'made' me share a testimony before the youth group; he begged me to be in the youth choir; he twisted my arm to give the devotional at a large youth gathering.

When I was getting ready to go to college, I was struggling to understand my future. Lee Simmons allowed me to get close enough to him to catch his heart to make a difference in people's lives. Because he'd made the effort to deepen his relationship with me, I heard his prayers for people, saw him minister to people, and watched him agonize over people. He had something I wanted. Yet, I did not think I had what it would take to succeed in ministry.

So, when I sensed God speaking to me about going into ministry, Lee was the first person I sought out for confirmation. I'll never forget what he said, "Dave, I believe God will use you to make a difference for Him." I wonder if I'd have become a pastor if it hadn't been for his encouragement. We all need someone to believe in us.

When I was a college student, I sensed God calling me to plant a church. Dr. Elmer Towns was one of the few people who expressed belief in my ability to plant a successful church. This was a giant encouragement I desperately needed. I wonder if I'd have become a church planter if it hadn't been for his encouragement. We all need someone to believe in us.

Encourage potential leaders by believing in them. Tell them when they're doing a good job. Point out everything they did right. Encourage them by helping them with some part of the process—like making copies of song sheets or ice breakers for them. Encourage them by speaking highly of them in front of the group. Ask God to guide you into the best way to encourage them.

Fill Their Tanks

When my boys were little, they had a toy lawn mower. When my oldest son was about three, he was in the phase of doing everything Dad did. One extremely hot Saturday afternoon, I got out my big mower. He got out his little mower. I pulled the string to start my mower. He pulled the imaginary string to start his. I began to cut the grass, and he followed behind me, pushing his mower.

When my mower stopped, he stopped. When I pulled the string and nothing happened, he pulled the imaginary string on his mower and nothing happened. When I kicked my mower, he kicked his mower. When I finally figured out I was out of gas and poured some gas into my mower, he poured imaginary gas into his mower.

I was reminded of two lessons that day. First, be careful what you say when you kick the lawn mower, because little ears are going to hear it and little boys may say it too. Second, engines won't work without fuel.

Since then I've been reminded that in some ways relationships are like engines. They also don't go far without emotional fuel. However, when the tanks are full, relationships go well, and advice and instruction are easily received. When the tanks are low, relationships and development efforts sputter.

Wise multipliers work hard to keep the emotional tanks of their potential leaders on "full." There are many ways to do this, including:

Emotional Tanks Fillers

Acceptance

Acceptance is like a magnet. It attracts people to you. One of the awesome things about small groups is everyone can feel acceptance there. I help lead a group of ninth and tenth graders. One of the things I love about our group is that we have a wonderful mix of kids. Some are very popular at school and some are completely unknown. We have clean-cut athletes, young men with long scraggly hair, and straight "A" marching band kids. We have one girl who dyes her hair a different neon color every few weeks and one young man who failed every class his first time through ninth grade. And they all feel acceptance from one another. As a result, they keep coming back and bringing their friends.

Every potential leader is different. Each of us has different strengths and weaknesses. We all have different personalities. Be certain to communicate acceptance to potential leaders and they'll be attracted to you. If you don't have this attitude naturally, ask God for it. He is an accepting God (He accepted me and you). He can give you His heart of acceptance for people.

Attention

When children's tanks are low, they show it. Often, they do things to get attention. When I was in first grade, I had a friend who was a very bright, athletic kid. But he was kind of lost in the shuffle of his parents' divorce. One day he coerced me into joining him in swinging around the boys' bathroom from stall to stall screaming like a monkey. Naturally, a teacher heard us and we got sent to the principal's office. He asked my friend why he'd done such a thing. He smiled and simply said, "To get attention."

Of course, most of your leaders won't play the fool (or) act silly to get your attention. But that doesn't mean they don't need it. In order to help keep the tanks of our potential leaders full, we need to give them attention. It doesn't usually take very long, but it does make a big difference.

Learn to be the giver of attention. Look at people when they speak. Read between the lines when they share concerns. Show interest in their jobs, their families, and their health. Ask about their day. Notice if they seem distracted or down. Pay more attention to them and they'll pay more attention to you.

Affirmation

Affirming others builds relationships and motivates better performance. A principal called some of his teachers aside and told them they'd been selected for a special assignment. He said they were exceptional teachers and would be given an exceptional group of students to teach that school year. The teachers rose to the challenge and taught at a higher level. They positively pushed their students to outstanding performance. At the end of the year the results were obvious, in that their students had excelled, finishing well above average.

The principal called those teachers back together and told them he had to make a confession. They and their students had been randomly selected. Going into the year neither they nor their students had performed exceptionally well on their test scores, but the affirmation of them as teachers and their students produced exceptional results.

Affirm your potential leaders. Go out of your way to express confidence in them. Show public trust in their abilities and character. Affirm their passion, skills, and efforts.

Affection

I spent one year training a pilot group of small group leaders. All the men in my group were older than I and already very committed Christians. One man had grown up in an alcoholic home, and affection was a very difficult thing for him. He was usually critical of what I was doing as a young pastor. He also worked with our teenagers and was critical of our youth pastor as well. So the youth pastor and I decided to try to "love him out of it." We both began to give him more affection. Our youth pastor took the physical approach by hugging him, and I took the verbal approach.

One night, I was giving him a ride home from our group. As he got out of the car I said, "Don't forget, I love you, man." He just looked at me and got out.

The next week, I said the same thing. "Don't forget, I love you, man."

He paused for awhile, then slowly said, "Well. My wife likes your wife a lot." And got out.

The next week I said it again. "Don't forget, I love you, man."

He looked at me and took a deep breath and said, "My wife and I like you and your wife too."

The next week I gave it another shot. "Don't forget, I love you, man."

He dropped his head and I noticed a tear on his cheek. Our youth pastor had been doing the same thing, and the power of affection was getting through.

"I, uh," he stammered and gulped hard, "I love you too."

After that he was a different man. He was still very disciplined and highly committed. But the hard edge had been replaced with warmth. He went from being a critic to an advocate. In fact he later moved to another state and drove his new pastor to distraction telling him all the good things our youth pastor and I were doing.

Learn to give your potential leaders appropriate affection. It fills their tanks and enhances your relationship. Tell them. Show them. An appropriate handshake, pat on the back, or hug will go a long way in letting people know you love them.

Activities

A good rule of thumb is to never do ministry alone. Whenever possible do things together. I travel and minister with a degree of frequency. I've learned to take the important people in my life with me. My last trip I took my middle son, who is also an apprentice for my high school group. The trip before that I went with two young church planters I try to mentor. My next trip, I'll take my wife.

Try to do ministry together. Visit the hospital, do follow-up, and pray together. Go to training classes or seminars together.

Try to have fun together. Sometimes it's not important what you do, but that you do it together. Some of our male leaders love to eat breakfast, golf, go to a ball game, or fish together. Some of our lady leaders enjoy shopping, cooking, or decorating together. The guys on our staff like to play basketball together. We used to play paint ball and disc golf together. A few times we went bowling or played board games.

It does not always matter what you do as much as that you do it together. Doing activities together fills tanks and deepens relationships.

Assistance

Bonds are created when we help each other. I'm not good at home repairs, so I deeply appreciate the guys who give me assistance with them. I'm a klutz with computers, so I appreciate people like Jack who help make my work easier. I'm better at coaching kids, so guys appreciate it when I pick their sons to be on my team and make them assistant coaches.

Look for ways to help out. Some of our leaders have built bridges to their potential leaders by baby-sitting for them, helping them balance their checkbooks, or assisting them in moving from one home to another. Assistance fills tanks and deepens relationships.

Learn to Listen

Years ago I was training a potential leader in my church. I can be a strong personality and a poor listener. One time, he was trying to share his heart with me, but I really wasn't listening. I thought I already knew what he was saying, but later I realized I was wrong. It was too late. The man was hurt by my failure to listen and dropped out of leadership training. He later left our church. We both were very hurt through the situation and I determined to become a better listener.

I've been married to Cathy for more than two decades. Our marriage keeps getting better and better. This is in part because I've learned to become a better listener. One of the best ways to deepen relationships is by listening.

I didn't become a better listener until I was convinced of the value of listening. I've noticed that people gravitate to good listeners and move away from poor listeners. To have a strong enough relationship with your potential leaders to influence them, you must become a good listener.

People need to feel heard before they're able to hear.

As leaders, we often talk too much and communicate too little. If we learn to listen better, what we *do* say will be more readily 'heard' and willingly applied. As a pastor, I've had many opportunities to deal with people who are very upset. I've learned that once I let them talk for awhile and make the effort to listen, they calm down. Then, and not before then, they're ready to hear my point of view.

We have to listen if we hope to really know what's going on.

People will tell you all sorts of things if you listen. Your potential leaders have much they'd love to share with you, and much that you need to know, if you're to effectively help them. They'll share it, but only if they know you'll listen.

Listening is essential for effective leading.

"The one skill that all great leaders recognize as indispensable to influence people and succeed … is the ability to listen."[1] Woodrow Wilson said, "The ear of the leader must ring with the voices of the people."[2]

Where I usually get in trouble trying to help potential leaders is where I go on a prescribed path without getting their feedback. Now, I try to get their ideas about everything coming along in the future of our group. This includes everything from what social activities we need to plan, to what the Bibles studies should be, to when we should multiply the group. We don't necessarily do everything they suggest—ninth graders have some nutty ideas—but most of what they say is right on track. They point out things I'd never notice if I hadn't been listening.

Listening shows you care.

Psychologist Joyce Brothers said, "Listening, not imitation, is the sincerest form of flattery." Dale Carnegie said, "You can make more friends in two weeks by becoming a good listener than you can in two years trying to get other people interested in you." If for no other reason, listening is valuable because it shows you care. It shows others that you care about their ideas, their feelings, and their opinions.

Tips for Effective Listening:

1. Concentrate on the people speaking.
2. Ask questions to probe their hearts.
3. Look at them.
4. Don't interrupt them.
5. Suspend judgment until they're done.
6. Briefly comment on what they're saying.
7. Repeat what you understand them to be saying back to them in your own words.
8. Ask questions to aid clarity.

If I could do anything to improve as a leader, it would be to go back and better apply this chapter to every potential leader I've tried to help. More of my failures have been because of neglecting the principles of deepening relationships than any other area.

I'm in ministry today because a youth pastor took the time and trouble to build a relationship with me. He cared. He filled my tanks. He listened. Because he cared for me, I learned to care for others and about ministry. I wonder how many lives you can influence through deepening relationships. I wonder how many potential leaders you can influence more effectively by deepening your relationship with them.

The Multiplying Leader's Deepening the Relationship Worksheet

The elements I am doing well are:

The elements in which I need to improve are:

The "tank-filling" efforts I regularly make are:

The efforts in which I need to do more are:

My potential leaders would say I'm a good
listener: True or False?

Which of the "Tips for Effective Listening" can I use
to improve my listening skills:

DESCRIBE:

Describe the Dream

Mike and Lois's group had bumped along for about a year and was just starting down the ugly process of becoming ingrown. Then Mike caught the dream of multiplication and began to pass it on to his group. He was very intentional about discussing the dream every single week, taking time to describe the vision of growth, health, and multiplication.

After some initial resistance, the group began to catch the dream. A few of the men began to meet with Mike for discipleship and training in leadership. Within a year, Tim and Rebecca launched a new group out of Mike's group with the same dream of multiplication. Soon there'll be three groups out of Mike's original group. Mike says it would have never happened if he hadn't regularly described the dream.

> The fifth step for developing new small group leaders is describing the vision.

One of the most important tools in the tool kit of the multiplying leader is describing the dream. You can have a big, powerful dream of multiplying your life, but unless and until you pass the dream of multiplication on to someone else, you'll never multiply. The dream will end with you.

Why Describe the Dream

A described dream attracts people

At the beginning of the 1992 presidential campaign, everyone expected incumbent President George Bush to easily win reelection. He'd won an astoundingly easy victory in the Desert Storm war with Iraq and was known as a man of integrity. But as the economy dipped, he failed to practice an essential for effective leadership. He failed, and later refused, to articulate a clear vision. Unlike his predecessor, Ronald Reagan, Bush failed to describe the dream of a better America.

This was especially fatal as his opponent, Bill Clinton, did one thing very well. He described his dream. In November 1992, when the final votes were in, the results were surprising. Because Clinton had described his dream and Bush refused to discuss the "vision thing," Clinton had won. Regardless of political persuasion, the lesson is clear. Describing a dream attracts followers. Failing to describe the dream keeps people from following a leader.

George Barna is adamant about the importance of having and describing a dream if you're to be effective as a leader. He writes, "Most people want to be led, but they will not voluntarily follow someone they deem unworthy of their support. In essence, they will refuse to place their trust and future in the hands of an alleged leader who does not possess vision."[1]

A described dream produces leaders.

Listeners are turned into learners, learners are turned into leaders, and leaders are turned into multipliers through hearing and having a dream. It's very difficult to produce leaders in a climate that lacks vision.

I attended a college founded by a man of incredible vision. He started a church with a handful of people that grew to thousands. The college grew from a few students to hundreds to thousands. He constantly spoke of the vision to capture a city for Christ. Hundreds of us caught the vision and went out to capture our towns for Christ. We weren't given the dream of survival but of citywide revival. Dozens of us started churches that are now the leading churches in our towns. The reason this happened was because our founder was always describing his dream and calling us to get our own dream of making a difference.

A described dream compels action and builds momentum.

Our church is in the process of planting churches and we're students of church planting. One thing we've found to be true all over the world is that without a described dream a church planter will never get a church off the ground. All things being equal, the church planter who can, and does, effectively describe the dream of the new church will succeed, where those who don't describe the dream well, or often, will fail.

This is true because the described dream creates the momentum necessary to break through mindsets and growth barriers. New churches in our part of the country need to average at least sixty people their first month to have the necessary momentum to move into viability. If they don't have sixty, the odds of them ever getting beyond it are slim. New small groups seem to need at least six to have the momentum to move into health, sustained growth, and multiplication. Of course there are exceptions to these numbers, but they're rare.

In a trip to the moon, a rocket will use most of its fuel breaking out of the earth's atmosphere. In launching a new group or a new church, the principle is the same. You must start well, with maximum momentum, or you'll never break out of the atmosphere. Maximum momentum is mandatory at the beginning. And, without an effectively described vision, there'll be little momentum. "When you don't have a vision, you don't produce anything."[2]

A described dream gives the sense that we're going somewhere.

A businessman got saved and spent a year or so in a traditional Sunday School class. He began to get bored and only went because his wife shamed him to attend. Then they moved to our city and began to attend our church. A leader invited him to a small group. The man was hesitant and skeptical. The leader asked him if he had any questions about going to a group. The man looked at his wife and gave her a mischievous grin. He finally had his chance and said, "I only have one question about your small group: do people ever graduate?"

"Yes," replied the leader with a confident smile, "They graduate into leading their own group!"

Without a vision the people lose interest or go to sleep or wander off. People love to feel they're part of something that's going somewhere. They want to feel they can get on board and be a part of something that has a future, a purpose, and is making a difference.

A described dream raises morale.

The second law of thermodynamics states that: all living things constantly move from a state of organization and energy to a state of disorganization and lethargy. This is true of everything, including your group. One way to combat this law is to describe the dream. Remind them of the big picture and the great purpose. A simple law of leadership is that you can raise morale when you can convey the vision.

As a pastor I've learned I must regularly speak of the 20,000 non-churched people in our town and the 850,000 non-churched people in our metropolitan area. I must show how, week-by-week, month-by-month, and year-by-year, we're making progress at reaching the lost for Christ.

A described dream inspires resolve and encourages people to sacrifice for a larger cause.

In 1940, Hitler quickly defeated France and seemed to have a clear path to take all of Europe. Germany immediately began preparing to invade England. The United States was far from being prepared to help, and it was expected that Great Britain, poorly armed and equipped, would fall in a few weeks. Yet, against the terrible possibility of a German invasion stood a man with the ability to describe a dream.

Winston Churchill took to the radio waves to breathe hope into his dispirited and frightened people. They gathered to hear him thunder out such words of inspiration as these:

> "I expect that the Battle of Britain is about to begin. Upon this battle depends the survival of Christian civilization. The whole fury and might of the enemy must soon be turned on us. Hitler knows that he must break us on this island or lose the war ... "Let us therefore brace ourselves to our duties and so bear ourselves that, if the British Empire and its Commonwealth last for a thousand years, men will still say, 'This was their finest hour!'"[3]

The people believed his words. They made tremendous sacrifices. They refused to give up. They fought back. And they kept Germany from successfully invading Britain.

Looking back at the way England stood against the fierce attacks testifies to the fact that, in many ways, it was their finest hour and a hinge on which Hitler's defeat swung. Historians agree that the reason the British people had the resolve to stand was because they had a leader whose descriptions of the dream would not let them give in.

Multiplying a small group isn't easy or automatic. Leaders must sacrifice. They must keep at it even when it's difficult. A dream motivates us to keep going and make the needed sacrifices to multiply the multipliers.

How to Describe the Dream

Get with God to receive a definite dream for multiplying your group that ties directly into the vision of your church.

This summer, as I thought about launching a new group for high school students, I spent time praying each day to ask God what He had in mind. He didn't speak to me in an audible voice or through a mystical vision, but as I prayed two pictures came to mind. First, my house was full of high school kids connecting with God every week. Second, the group multiplied every year for several years until four to eight such groups were meeting all over the area, and all this happened before my ninth grade son graduated.

George Barna wrote the book on vision (literally ... it's called *The Power of Vision*). He defines vision as: "a specific, detailed, customized, distinctive and unique notion of what you are seeking to do to create a particular outcome."[4]

He continues, "So what is vision? It is a clear mental portrait of a preferable future, communicated by God to His chosen servant-leaders, based upon an accurate understanding of God, self, and circumstances."[5] " ... vision is a clear compelling picture of a better tomorrow, that inspires people to change, to get involved, to care and to do things that contribute to the common good."[6]

Barna adds that, "True vision comes from God."[7] He cautions that "Gaining the vision is simple, but it is not quick ... I firmly believe that God takes greater pleasure in the process of working with us to get the vision than He takes in us finally attaining it."[8]

If you don't have a definite dream, let me give you some examples:

• Lead a healthy growing multiplying group.
• Mentor a new leader and multiply a resulting new group every year.
• Spend the next five years training five multipliers, one each year.
• Spend the rest of your life finding and training a group of twelve multipliers.

Tell the dream to the key people involved. Let them add to it and own it. Specify the potential leader's possible role in the dream.

After I got the dream of a high school group where kids would meet God every week and the group would multiply every six to twelve months, I began to share it with the key people needed to make the dream become a reality. First I discussed it with my wife Cathy, since it would meet at our house. Then I described it to my son Andrew, who'd be my apprentice, then to Ed, who'd become my adult apprentice and eventually the adult leader of the second group, then to my son's friend Adam, who'd be the apprentice to become the student leader of the second group.

As I shared my dream, they added their personal twists, and it became *our* dream. Andrew and I had just returned from a few days of prayer-saturated ministry at a Christian university, when he added that the group should be saturated in prayer, and he volunteered to lead a prayer meeting each week before the group meeting to pray for the group. Cathy added the desire to make the group very biblical, since kids in our culture know so little about the Bible. Ed wanted it to have definite direction, so that it wouldn't be a waste of time.

Next we shared with a second level of leaders, four students Andrew and Adam recruited to help lead. We talked about their possible role in leading their own groups in the future. We let them add to and own the vision as well. For example, Daniel stressed the desire to see lost kids coming and getting saved. Another student (who is also named Andrew) wanted to be sure it was fun.

In two weeks, the dream of a multiplying high school group had gone from *my* dream to *our* dream. Because it is our dream, we've all worked to make it succeed. Within weeks we were averaging almost thirty students each week who break into five small groups for discussion and prayer.

Write a dream statement that will clarify and direct what you're trying to do.

Barna writes, "For the vision to be effective … it must be simple enough to be remembered and specific enough to give direction."[9] Our group is at the point of needing to write a mission or dream statement that will clarify and direct what we are trying to do.

"S.M.A.R.T." dream statements contain five elements. They are:

- S: Specific.
- M: Measurable.
- A: Attainable
- R: Relevant
- T: Time-oriented

This statement should be a brief, memorable descriptive in no more than two sentences. For example, we may define our dream as: "To be a growing, prayer-saturated group where high school students gather weekly to meet with God and each other and to multiply at least every year."

It's specific. It tells who'll be involved: *high school students*. It describes what they'll do: *gather weekly to meet with God and each other and to multiply at least every year*. It tells what will be a key element of making that happen: *a growing, prayer-saturated group*.

It's measurable: We can ask at the end of each week these questions of measurement:

- Did we saturate the group with prayer?
- Are we reaching new people?
- Did we meet with God?
- Did we have positive fellowship with each other?
- Are we taking steps toward multiplying in a year?

It's attainable. So far we've done well each week when compared with the five measuring questions. We'll know for sure in a year if we really succeeded at the fifth one, but we are taking steps.

It's relevant. Our vision statement conveys elements of the deep desires of everyone on our leadership team. It meets needs in our community. It makes a difference in the lives of students.

It's time-oriented. The statement says: *to multiply at least every year*. This is a very important component because it speaks of multiplication and gives a date for accomplishing it. Our size may cause us to multiply sooner, but we want to make sure the leadership team of the second group and future groups will be strong before they launch. Having a year is a challenging yet attainable time frame in our context.

We may tweak the statement as we go. We may want to be more specific about reaching the lost or training both student and adult leaders.

Share the vision.

Too often leaders define their dream and don't spend enough time sharing it. The dream will not accomplish all it can unless it's shared. It won't attract followers or produce leaders. It can't compel action or build morale. It won't give a sense of direction. It can't inspire resolve and encourage sacrifice unless and until it's shared.

It only makes sense. A mediocre dream that's shared will always accomplish more than a great dream not shared at all. People need to hear the dream described enough to be able to recite it back. They need to have it described for them enough that they know what it means and where they fit into it. They need to hear it often enough that they can share it with others.

Share the dream all the time.

George Barna makes a profound statement when he asks the question, "When should the vision be communicated to people? At every opportunity."[10] Mike, the group leader I referred to at the beginning of the chapter, has been successful at multiplying his group because, week after week, he has described his dream of reaching out and multiplying his group. One of my weaknesses as a leader is that I don't describe the vision often enough.

In 1980, Paul Yonggi Cho's church had 150,00 members. Yet his vision at that time called for 500,000. At the beginning of 1981, he said, "I am constantly speaking about those 500,000 members."[11] He also said a leader must "persuade the congregation of the reality of that goal and get some enthusiasm started. By constantly speaking about my goal and my visions, I am generating enthusiasm in the people and persuading them that it is going to happen."[12]

Share the dream in as many mediums as possible.

There are many mediums in which to share the dream. The wise leader will use as many as possible. Some effective ways of sharing the dream include story-telling, slogans, signs or banners, or even songs that promote it. Publicly teach on it, pray about it, and note any progress in fulfilling it. Write about it in a letter. Refer to it in a conversation. Mention it in a testimony.

Share the dream in as many ways as possible.

There are many ways to share the dream. The wise leader will use as many as possible. Some effective ways of sharing the dream include:

• Be Passionate

This was Martin Luther King's secret for inspiring action. When he stood on the steps of the Lincoln Memorial and cried, "I have a dream!" his voice shook with passion and conviction. As a result, the world shook with his dream of equal rights.

If you're not excited about it, no one else will be. Howard Hendricks used to say, "If you want your audience to bleed, you will have to hemorrhage." Say it with passion. As Barna remarks, "What makes a vision most attractive is fervor."[13]

• *Be Relevant*

Every hearer asks the same question of every message: "What's in it for me?" Show the hearers where they fit. Tell them how it will benefit their lives. Point out the attractive elements of the dream.

Often small groups resist multiplication because it's presented as the painful division of friendships. Wise leaders always speak in positive, not negative terms. It's multiplication, not division. It's a chance to make new friends and reach new people who wouldn't be reached any other way. They speak in terms of the big picture itself, not of selfish agendas. Multiplication of new groups is an opportunity for more people to step up their impact. It's God's plan to reach the world and build His kingdom.

• *Be Confident*

I tend to be negative, fearful, and overly analytical. But I've found that the secret of self-confidence is God-reliance. Paul said, "I can do all things through Christ who gives me strength" (Phil. 4:13). If it's from God, it will happen. If God leads us and helps us do the right things, it will be accomplished.

Group members radiate the level of confidence the leader reflects. Whenever you speak of the dream, do so with confidence in them, in God, and in what He will do through them.

• *Be Humble*

People are turned off by arrogance. And God resists pride. But confident humility is another thing. As we've said, self-confidence is based on God-reliance. It's saying, "I can't, but God can and will do it." Share the dream with a 'God and others' focus.

• *Share Publicly and Privately*

Much of what we've said relates to the public setting. But don't overlook the power of the private, dream-casting experience. There's something powerful about looking others in the eye and sharing with passion and confident humility that God is going to do great things. And they can be a big part of it.

"My experience in studying the transfer of vision from the visionary to his followers is that people are most likely to buy the vision when they have an intimate meeting with the visionary."[14]

Keep sharing the dream.

One of my biggest challenges is to keep sharing the dream even after I've gotten tired of hearing myself speak of it. I have to remind myself that everyone hasn't heard this as many times as I have. Other people have to think about many other things that tend to crowd out the dream. I need to keep on saying it to remind them what it's all about. I have to reinforce its importance again and again.

The Elim church in El Salvador has almost 50,000 members. They have a systematic aid in reminding themselves of their vision. Every week the members repeat their five-fold purpose statement. As a result of such attention to sharing the dream they have over 130,000 people in groups. [15]

The Multiplying Leader's "Describe the Dream" Worksheet

I have a definite dream for my group. True or False?
My dream is:

I need to get with God to get a definite dream for multiplying my group.
True or False?
If not, I will do this (when):

I've described the dream to the key people involved, allowing them to add to it and own it. True or False?
If not, I will do this (when):

I've written a dream statement that's specific, measurable, attainable, relevant, time-oriented, and that clarifies and directs what we're trying to do. True or False?
It is:

I've shared the dream with my group. True or False?
If not, I will do this (when):

I need to share the dream more often. True or False?
If, true, I will do this (when):

I need to share the dream using more mediums. True or False?
If true, I will do this (when):

I need to share the dream more passionately, relevantly, confidently, humbly, publicly, and privately. True or False?
If true, I will do this (when):

I need to share the dream more persistently. True or False?
If true, I will do this (when):

DETERMINE:

Determine Expectations and Commitments

A Quick Learner

Ted was one of the easiest potential leaders I've ever mentored. I'd watched him for about seven months and thought he had great potential. For several months I prayed about an apprentice before I approached him about it. He was very bright and had a warm heart. He had good people awareness and a desire to do things right.

After group one night we talked briefly about the possibility of him becoming an apprentice in my group. I gave him a one-page description of what would be expected of him and asked him to read it. Later, we sat down for lunch and I explained each part of the expectations. He made some notes, listened intently, and asked for clarifications. When he left he agreed to pray about it and discuss it with his wife.

> The sixth step for developing new group leaders is determining expectations and commitments.

When we got together a week or so later, he said he and his wife had agreed that the Lord was leading him in this direction and wanted to give it a try. That week he began weekly calls to the members of our group. He began praying for them daily. I slowly gave him responsibilities such as leading the icebreaker, the prayer time, or the Bible discussion. I talked to him on the phone almost every week and at church on Sundays. He was an avid learner and took the training classes offered by our church.

Ted was a quick learner. Within a few months he was leading his own group and doing a good job.

I wish I had spent more time with Ted because I really like him. But our schedules at that time prohibited it from happening. But he was such a quick learner that once he had the expectations and commitments made clear, he had the main puzzle pieces needed to move toward and into leadership.

With Ted I was reminded of a valuable lesson. In developing leaders it's essential to clearly determine expectations and commitments. One of the biggest oversights we tend to have in developing leaders is not taking the time early in the relationship to determine expectations and commitments.

What Determines Expectations and Commitments

Clearly determined and agreed-upon expectations and commitments give both the potential leader and the mentoring leader direction.

My oldest son runs cross-country. I love the start of a big cross-country meet. I love the pent-up tension of hundreds of runners waiting for the signal to go. Then, once the gun goes off, the colorful pack springs forward as hundreds of runners desperately look ahead to make sure they're going down the right path. Good potential leaders are like good cross-country runners. They'll run hard if they're confident they're going in the right direction.

Leroy Eims of The Navigators has written, "A leader is one who sees more than others see, who sees further than others see, and sees before others see."[1] John Maxwell has written that a person of influence navigates for other people.[2] I find most potential leaders will do an outstanding job if they have sufficient direction. Taking the time and trouble to determine expectations and commitments gives them direction.

Clearly determined and agreed upon expectations and commitments limit frustrations.

One of the most frustrating years of my life was spent working without a job description. I was hired as the director of discipleship for a large Christian university. My boss was spread very thin and never took the time to even give me a job description, even though I asked for it on several occasions. Eventually he got tired of me asking and said, "Just write your own."

So I did, but I was still frustrated. He wasn't doing what I'd hoped when I took the job, and I wasn't doing what he hoped when he hired me. I put my focus on developing three hundred small prayer and discipleship groups for our 2,500 on-campus students. I spent time writing curricula, training the leaders, and training the leaders of the leaders.

Later I found out he wanted me to be doing a campus radio program and developing a workshop on rock music. I wanted him to mentor me in leadership and take me with him on his preaching trips, and he wanted me to free him up by helping teach his classes. We were frustrated with each other for a year, simply because clarifications and commitments were never determined.

The next year my boss was promoted and I got a new boss. We sat down and together we determined exactly what was expected of me. My productivity, confidence, and fulfillment improved. My boss was happy and so was I.

Clearly determined and agreed upon expectations and commitments aid communication.

There may be times when an apprentice isn't doing what we expect. If expectations and commitments have been agreed upon ahead of time, the leader can simply remind the apprentice of the expectations. But if the expectations haven't been determined, disappointment and the resulting withdrawal can occur. Communication will be limited.

This can work both ways. When the mentoring leader isn't meeting the expectations of the apprentice, he or she can get disappointed and withdraw as well. This is avoidable when expectations and commitments are clearly defined, determined, and discussed ahead of time. The door of communication is opened and is more easily kept open.

Clearly determined and agreed upon expectations and commitments provide motivation.

Many people lack faith in themselves. They may not have someone who believes in them. But when someone comes along who does believe in them, they take notice. They'll give great effort in trying to live up to those expectations.

I have seen this happen repeatedly when I coach sports. I remember one tall eight-year-old boy named Jason who was having trouble hitting. After two games he had seven strikeouts in seven at bats. He was swinging properly but was just not hitting the ball. He lacked confidence.

One evening before the game he told me his dad was coming to watch him play, and he hoped he'd get a hit. He said his dad told him he expected him to get a hit that night.

Before he went to bat, I grabbed his shoulders and looked him in the eye. "*After* you hit the ball and run to first base" I said, "watch the coach. If he's waving you on around first base keep going hard, straight to second base. We expect you to hit a double tonight." He nodded his head and gave me a big smile. I called after him, "*After* you hit it, watch the coach." Then I prayed really hard.

On the first pitch, Jason swung with confidence and drove the ball into the outfield. He tore down first and raced into second base. Then he stood there with a confident grin on his face. His dad and I were also smiling. Jason had the ability all the time. He just needed to know that people believed in him and that he could be expected to succeed. Jason became a steady doubles hitter all year.

Clearly determined and agreed upon expectations and commitments help give potential leaders a tool to later use in developing their own leaders.

Bill Bright has built the largest ministry in the world, Campus Crusade for Christ, in part, on the principle of transferable concepts. The idea is that resources are developed with the mindset that they need to be transferable from one person to another. Person A will take person B through the materials. Then person B will transfer them to person C. Then person C will teach them to person D and so on.

Remember, the goal is to multiply leaders who will multiply leaders. We need to give our potential leaders the principles and tools they can use in the future with their potential leaders.

How to Determine Expectations and Commitments

Often your church, pastor, small groups pastor, or coach has already prepared standard expectations and commitments. If so, use them. If not, get some from an effective small group ministry in your area.

There are often two levels of expectations and commitments. The first level is for people who are just "trying on" group leadership. This would be a new apprentice. The second level would be for the person who's successfully fulfilling the first level commitments and is rapidly heading for the leadership of a group. It might be helpful if I explain the expectations and commitments we use.

Basic Level Commitment:
Expect them to set the PACE

I ask new apprentices to make a simple fourfold commitment using the acrostic P.A.C.E.:

P: Prayer. Pray for group members daily. I usually give them four to ten names of group members they're to pray for daily. This gives them a heart for the people. It increases God's working in the group members' lives. And it frees the mentoring leader from needing to pray for too many people. I generally only pray for my apprentices.

A: Availability. Be available to group members outside the group setting. I have a strong personality as a leader. In order to multiply I must wean group members from me as quickly as possible. I also want to build the bridge between apprentice and group members as quickly as possible. I have my apprentices give their phone numbers to the group members they're praying for each day. I expect them to be the first ones to visit those people if they have to go to the hospital.

C: Contact. Contact the group members weekly. I expect my apprentices to make a five-minute phone call to each of the people they're praying for every week. This keeps the apprentices in touch with the people for whom they're praying. It helps the group members feel that someone cares for them. It builds the relationships that pave the way for the eventual multiplication of the group. And it frees the leader from calling all the group members. The leader needs to call only the apprentices.

During the call they may ask things like:

"How are you doing?"

"What can I pray for you about?"

"What did you like about the group last night?"

"Have you ever thought about becoming an apprentice?"

"What week was it that you wanted to bring refreshments?"

"We've been praying for your friend at work. Did she say if she was coming to church this week or not?"

They may also say things like:

"I want you to know I really appreciated what you shared last week in our group."

"I want to remind you to put our group party on your calendar."

"Let me tell you that as I pray about people to become my apprentices when our group multiplies, your name keeps coming to mind."

E: Example. Apprentices are expected to be examples. When you start talking about being an example, some people get intimidated. So, we speak of being examples of progressing Christians, not perfect ones. How you define a progressive Christian will be different in different settings. In this context, I'm generally expecting examples in things such as daily Bible reading and prayer, church attendance, and often reading a book I've given them.

Make the commitment to set the P.A.C.E. for them. You can't expect your leaders to set the pace for others if you're not willing to set the pace for them. When expectations and commitments are being determined, tell them they can expect you to set the pace for them. Make the commitment to pray for them daily, be available to them, call them weekly, and be an example to them.

Advanced Level Commitment

Expect them to become "Eight Habits" leaders.

In the chapter on Demonstration, I mentioned the eight habits of effective leaders. (A detailed and highly practical description of each of these habits is found in the book, *8 Eight Habits of Effective Small Group Leaders*, published by Cell Group Resources, 2001.)[3]

I'm currently helping to lead a group for high school students. I spent August training my apprentices to be "Eight Habits" leaders. The group began in September. Because we did most of the habits most of the time the group grew and the apprentices developed to the point that we successfully multiplied into two groups in January.

I'm currently taking my next batch of apprentices through the Eight

Habits. As they're doing them, our group has grown. It looks like we'll be able to successfully multiply again as soon as summer or as late as September.

1. Dream. Write out specific goals for the growth and multiplication of the group you lead. Ask the members to dream of leading their own healthy, growing, multiplying group one day. When they're ready, jointly set a date for the multiplication of the present group. This would be the birth date of their own group.

2. Pray for your group members, group apprentice(s), and group multiplication daily. They're already doing this under their PACE commitment.

3. Invite new people to your group weekly. They need to develop the habit of inviting new people now. If they don't learn to invite new people, the group they one day lead won't grow.

4. Contact group members regularly. They're already doing this under their PACE commitment.

5. Prepare for your group meeting. Explain that they'll begin to have weekly assignments for various parts of the group meeting. These could include the opening prayer, the announcements, the prayer time, the icebreaker, the testimony, or the Bible lesson/ discussion. I start by giving them one element a week. They do it and then I give feedback and coaching. When they're handling it successfully, then I add another. Have them build into their schedule time to prepare for their part in the weekly group. Later, when they're ready to lead their own group, they already have preparation time in place.

6. Have and mentor apprentice leaders. They need to know they're expected to have at least one apprentice in place before they can open their own group. This will become a serious matter of prayer and discussion between you and them. It's a great day when your apprentices have their own apprentices and their apprentices are starting to set the PACE.

7. Plan group fellowship activities. Eventually give them at least one activity to plan and lead from start to finish before they open their own group.

8. Be committed to personal growth. This is where you might share with them that you expect them to meet with you regularly for training and coaching, to help them get ready to open their own group. My current group of apprentices and their apprentices meet together for training every Sunday evening for one hour before the evening service. We just finished reading the Eight Habits book and are now learning how to give personal testimonies. They need to be building time into their schedule to be trained and later to do training.

Leadership Expectations and Covenant

Developing some expectations and a covenant will greatly enhance your ability to raise up effective leaders. It's a goal to shoot for, a template to train toward, and a standard to ensure quality. A sample of such an agreement is below:

Group Leadership Agreement

In my desire to take on the responsibility of shepherding and caring for a small group,

I have:
❑ Prayed about the decision.
❑ Been a part of a small group.
❑ Developed a prospect list.
❑ Identified an apprentice and a host.
❑ Been approved by the appropriate authorities /pastor in our church.

I am:
❑ Willing to put down murmurings and be a team player.
❑ Willing to lead my group in outreach and incorporating new members into the group on a regular basis.
❑ Desirous of becoming a leader and a developer of leaders.

Signed:_____

Date:_____

Tie Into Your Church's Leadership Expectations

Most churches have some sort of leadership standards or covenant. It's good to make sure they're up to speed on these expectations before you get too far along in the mentoring process.

Closing the Sale and Drawing the Net

One day at lunch I was recruiting a new apprentice, a salesman. When I finished he looked at me and laughed. He said, "I mean this as a compliment. I've been in sales for twenty-five years. That was as good an appeal as I've ever heard. And I loved the way you closed the sale."

I'd never looked at it that way before. But if I had to "sell" something, I believe that small group leadership training is a very valuable commodity to have and to sell. As I thought about the methods of recruitment that worked, I realized there was truth in what he said. It's kind of like a salesman closing a sale. Or another image might be that recruiting a small group leader apprentice is similar to winning a person to Christ. It's like drawing the net when you "fish for men." The elements are similar:

1. Recruit to a vision, not to a job. Give him or her a vision of what they could accomplish as a multiplying leader.
2. Explain in sufficient detail the expectations and the commitments needed to be made to each other in order to make the relationship most effective.
3. Ask clarifying questions, such as:
   "Do you understand what's expected?"
   "What do you think of these expectations?"
   "Can you do these things at this time?"
   "Is there anything you can't fulfill at this time?"
   "Is anything keeping you from fulfilling these expectations?"
   "Is there anything you need from me beyond what we've discussed?"
4. Ask for the commitment. Sometimes in recruiting a potential leader, the mentoring leader makes the mistake of failing to ask for a commitment, perhaps thinking it's too pushy, or maybe too formal. But small group leadership is a very important responsibility. The fact that you're asking others to join you in the work of such importance demands an urgent appeal by you and a high-level commitment from them. So ask for it. I've asked such

closing questions as:
"Do you need to discuss this with (your mate, your parents, etc.) first or are you ready to make the commitment right now?"
"Are you ready to get started today?"
"Are you ready to seal this in prayer right now?"
"Can I count on you to be my apprentice?"
"Are you ready to sign up today to grow our group and multiply it?"
"Well, do I have a new apprentice?"

The Multiplying Leader's Determine Worksheet

- Do you have a written list of such things as an "Apprentice Expectations Description" and your church's leaders' covenant? Do you need to create them?

- If you have an apprentice, are you both clear on the expectations and commitments needed to make their training most effective?

  If not, what's your next step?

DEVELOP:

Develop the Potential Leader

It's Time to Multiply

I just read an e-mail from my friend Kent, who leads a small group at our daughter church. In less than a year his group has already successfully multiplied. In the e-mail he said that his "small" group wasn't small anymore, because they had thirty on hand the night before. Then he said, "I guess it's time to multiply again!"

Wow! What an exciting challenge it is to lead a healthy, growing group. But the real challenge is to be sure to have developed the potential leaders of new groups in order to prepare to multiply. Successful multiplication will never happen without developing potential leaders.

The Goal of Development

When I was the director of discipleship at a Christian university, I read everything I could about discipleship. I thought it was interesting that many writings focused on why and how to make a disciple, but never told how to know when you had made a disciple.

Let me be very clear on this point. The goal of developing disciples is to develop them to *do* something. In this book, the product of dreaming, discovering, and deepening activities is the development of leaders able to spearhead growing, healthy groups that are able to multiply. In other

The seventh step for developing new group leaders is developing them.

words, the goal is to develop small group leaders who'll develop other small group leaders. The goal is not to merely build a group. It's to build up multiplying small group leaders.

Joel Comiskey writes, "Cell reproduction is so central to a cell ministry that the goal of cell leadership is not fulfilled until the new groups are also reproducing—the theme of reproduction must guide cell ministry. The desired end is that each cell grows and multiplies."[1] He also states, "the principal job of the cell leader is to train the next cell leader—not just fill the house with guests."[2]

The Definition of Development

A definition of development, as described in this chapter, is:

Development is the process of cooperating with God by using every available resource to help another person become a multiplying small group leader.

Notice the various pieces of this definition:

First, it is a *process*, not an event. That means it takes time. It involves steps. It's taking someone from one level to another.

Second, it's *cooperating with God*. God is in the process of developing leaders. He works in ways that are deeper, more powerful and more effective than we could ever work on our own. He will use circumstances and events. He will use all elements of His body. The job of the multiplying leader is to simply cooperate with what God is already doing. This makes prayer a key component of the multiplying leader's tool kit.

Third, development is *using every available resource*. Some of the resources available to the multiplying leader include classes, on-the-job training, books, tapes, workbooks, and personal mentoring.

Fourth, it's *helping another person become a multiplying small group leader*. How do you know if you've done the job? The answer is obvious. The other person is effectively leading a group that's multiplying leaders.

Resources of Development

On-the-Job Training

The best and most basic way of developing a potential leader into an effective leader is on-the-job training. This works best when the leader delegates areas of responsibility to the potential leader and supervises how he or she does each of them. For example, the potential leader leads the prayer session for the group as the leader observes and later does an evaluation with the potential leader. The latter learns by doing ministry in a supervised setting.

Personal Mentoring and Coaching

This is a one-on-one meeting between the multiplying leader and the potential leader. Anything and everything could serve as the basis of discussion. But, the focus is most frequently on the elements of the on-the-job training process. For example, the multiplying leader tells the potential leader how to lead the prayer time. Then, after the potential leader has tried it, the multiplying leader provides feedback.

Classroom Training

This is a structured class that is most often taught by someone other than the multiplying leader. At our church, the small groups pastor teaches a four-hour class, which is required for all potential leaders before they lead a recognized group. There are also several classes they can take after they begin leading a group.

Group Leadership Training

If the multiplying leader has several potential leaders, they might meet regularly as a group for some type of training. The nature of this training could be decided by the multiplying leader and is based upon the need of their potential leaders. This may include reading a book together or practicing specific skills. All the potential leaders for my high school group meet together weekly. The first few weeks, we read and discuss a book about small group leadership. After that, we discuss how to share a three-minute testimony and take turns sharing them each week in the training session, before sharing them later in the week at the group session. This book serves as one of our discussion resources.

Training Events

Our small groups pastor schedules a one-day training event for group leaders every year. Touch Outreach Ministries in Houston, Texas offers some great seminars you can attend or host in your church.

Wasting Time Together

My friend, Jay Firebaugh, is an outstanding pastor of a strong cell church in Houston, Texas. He recently spoke at our church, and one of the many things he said that seemed to make a lasting impression on our small group leaders was the idea of small group members "'wasting time together."

We're all so busy doing what we think of as "ministry" that we often miss the real ministry that occurs when we simply "waste time together." Wasn't this often the primary method of Jesus? How many hours He must have spent just walking and talking with His disciples.

Books, Tapes, and Magazines

By using books, tapes, and magazines, your potential leaders can receive training from experts when you aren't around. There's a plethora of great resources available. Let me recommend the many books used in the endnotes of this book. Let me also encourage you to take advantage of the website <www.cellgrouppeople.com> for access to many other great books and resources. Also, many leaders are finding the value of reading and discussing a chapter a week of a helpful small group "how to" book.

Steps of Training Development.

I. Model it.

The multiplying leader does the activity and the potential leader watches. This could cover any or all of the activities needed to lead an effective group. These include leading the group icebreaker or prayer time, making phone calls to group members, planning and running a group social event, visiting a member in the hospital, or preparing the lesson.

These ministry activities may come easy for you now, but they're intimidating to a potential leader. De-mystify the activities for the potential leader by modeling them.

Never do ministry alone. Take your leaders with you. Let them see you doing it. Show them how it's done.

2. Mentor it.

The multiplying leader shows the potential leader how to do the activity and lets the potential leader do it as the leader watches. Afterward, the multiplying leader gives the potential leader needed encouragement and helpful feedback.

This could involve practice sessions or role-playing. Let them practice leading the icebreaker on you first. Let them practice leading the Bible discussion with you first. Let them role-play a phone call to a group member who was absent.

Then let them do it "live." I generally start apprentices off leading the prayer time. I have them ask the person to the left to share one current need, and then the potential leader should pray for that need immediately. Then have the next person share a need and the previous person pray for it immediately, continuing until everyone in the group has shared and prayed for each other.

3. Motivate it.

The multiplying leader steps away, allowing the potential leader to lead. This could range from being out of the room to being out of town.

I have several apprentices for my high school group. They're currently leading the prayer times for our group every week. After the lesson, I send them off with a bit of instruction and they each go to separate parts of the house with several students. They lead the prayer time, while I walk around and observe from a distance. I may give them some feedback and encouragement, usually later that week during our training session. But a quality prayer time is up to them.

4. Multiply it.

The potential leader consistently leads without the direct supervision of the multiplying leader. This could begin with making phone calls and leading the elements of the group meeting. Eventually, the potential leaders lead their own group and train their own potential leaders.

Putting the Four Steps Together

Here's an example of how this process might occur. Betty asks Debbie to be her apprentice. They'll meet the night before the group each week to pray for the group and prepare for the meeting.

Model it. Month one, Betty does all the preparing and leading and Debbie watches. Betty is careful to explain what, why, and how she's doing things as she goes.

Mentor it. Month two, Debbie prepares the icebreaker. She practices it in front of Betty, who makes some encouraging and helpful comments. Then Debbie leads the icebreaker in the group. Betty gives her more encouraging and helpful feedback when they get together in their weekly meeting.

Motivate it. Month three, Debbie does the icebreaker all by herself. Occasionally Debbie gives some encouraging or helpful feedback.

Multiply it. Month four, Debbie does the icebreaker.

If Betty's smart, she'll do basically the same thing with each of the pieces of group leadership until Debbie can do each group meeting element confidently by herself. As she's turning over the icebreaker, Betty may begin to take Debbie through the same steps with the prayer time. After that she may take her through these steps in training her to lead the Bible discussion.

Roles Needed for Development

Sometimes it's helpful to realize that the development process is aided when the mentoring leader is able to play more than one role in developing potential disciples. This isn't a formal type of thing, but rather a casual adaptation of style and approach in order to help give the potential leader what they may need. The role played by the multiplying leader changes to fit the experience, maturity and personality of the potential leader. These roles may include:

Discipler

The role of discipler is simply helping potential leaders grow in Christ. It centers on showing them the why and how of important holy habits like prayer, Bible reading, Bible study, journaling, fasting, and evangelism. The discipler is to be an *example of spiritual disciplines*, helping potential leaders grow in their spiritual life and holding them accountable for maintaining the disciplines of spiritual growth.

The primary way I play this role with the high school students who are my apprentices is by taking time every few weeks to ask them such questions as:

"What have you been reading in the Bible?"

"When do you do your Bible reading?"

"How has your prayer life been going lately?"

"Who have you invited to group in the last two weeks?"

"When was the last time you shared your faith at school and how did it go?"

Coach

The role of coach is to teach and train in skills, such as how to lead an effective icebreaker or to set up a successful activity. The coach role is one of *empowerment through training,* working through the Steps of Training Development as described earlier in the chapter.

Chris is helping me lead our high school group. As our group is getting nearer to the date for multiplying, he's taking a larger and larger role in leading the group. The other week he led the Bible discussion, and did a great job. After the group meeting, I took about ten minutes to share with him the three or four things I thought he did especially well. Then I shared the two things he probably could have done a bit better. Being a teachable emerging leader, he appreciated the feedback.

Counselor

By counselor, I don't mean something formal and long-term. The idea is that the multiplying leader is willing to give advice as needed to aid potential leaders through snags in their lives. It's sharing what has worked for you. It's giving them instruction, warning, advice, and accountability when appropriate. The counselor role is one of *exhortation.*

There are times when small group leaders need to back off and refer the person to a pastor or professional counselor. Perhaps you're not making any progress or the person is taking up too much of your time. Referral is especially important if the person is demonstrating serious behavorial problems, such as:

- Depression
- Extreme mood swings
- Violent outbursts of anger that harm others either physically or verbally
- Loss of contact with reality
- Serious, irrational fears
- Drug or alcohol abuse
- Child abuse or neglect
- A desire to hurt others

Teacher

The teacher role involves explaining needed information and leading to appropriate application. Topics included may be Bible doctrine or spiritual growth principles. The teacher role is one of *explanation and illustration.* Again this isn't a formal role. It may be as simple as taking a minute to clarify something that was said in the group. It could be taking a few minutes in your training time to demonstrate how you use a Bible commentary to aid your study.

Sponsor

The sponsor recognizes the potential of emerging leaders and gives them a chance to begin to lead. The sponsor role is one of *encouragement*. It begins when you help them take steps to becoming apprentices. It may lead to attending the first session of your church's leadership training course with them. It might involve helping them find an apprentice and a host home for the new group. It could mean helping recruit people to attend the new leader's group.

Most of us will find that we gravitate toward one role more than the others. Realize that all may be needed at one time or another. If you're not comfortable playing each role for the potential leader, someone needs to do so. Ask your coach or pastor to help if needed.

Suggestions for Effective Development

Have a weekly or twice a month meeting time with your apprentice(s).

I meet with apprentices an hour before church on Sunday evenings. We do things like discuss a chapter of a book, check up on personal growth plans, and debrief the previous week's group meeting. We may also plan an activity, discuss multiplication dates, or talk through possible future apprentices.

We may train in one of the skills needed to lead a group meeting, such as leading the prayer time. We go over the calendar of what we're studying and who's leading which aspect of the group the next few weeks. We may plan an upcoming activity. And we always pray for each other and the group.

This meeting need not last long, but it *is* essential. The more often you meet with and intentionally train your leaders, the more rapidly they'll be ready to lead an effective, growing multiplying group.

Use every possible resource (on-the-job training, personal meetings, classroom experiences, group training seminars, wasting time together, books, tapes, and magazines.)

Try to see that apprentices get at least one resource each week. Consider the resources to be like vitamins. The more they get, the healthier they'll be, and the faster they'll develop.

Claude and Ginny, the leaders of our singles small groups, are great at including their leaders in everything the church offers. They bring them to seminars, sign them up for classes, and get together for planning powwows. As a result, their ministry has grown from one other person to nine or ten groups in just a few years.

Try to do at least one step of training development with your potential leaders every time you meet.

Always be training in something. If it's not how to invite new people, then show them how to set up a personal growth plan. Pray with them for their apprentices. Show them how to set up an effective activity. If you meet weekly and give them at least one new thing every week, it will amaze you what they can learn in a year. This doesn't have to be long. Five or ten minutes at a time is often sufficient.

If you don't feel competent to train in an area, bring in your small group pastor or coach to help. Learn together by reading a book together. Go together to another small group leader's training session and learn from it.

Ask potential leaders what role they most want or need you to play for them at a given time.

I tend to think I know best, which is often not the case. I think they need a good dose of training, while they feel they need some counsel about a situation at work with their boss. People learn best when they're motivated to learn. The best way to help potential leaders grow is to cooperate with their current motivations.

I've learned to ask the people I mentor a question that's extremely helpful. I may phrase it differently, but the idea is the same:

"What is it that I can do to help you reach your goal?"
"What area in your leadership would you most like me to help you with?"
"What do you most need from me right now?"

Ask yourself every week, "What can I do to help my potential leader be better prepared to lead a healthy, growing, multiplying group?"

This may only take a few minutes, but it will be very helpful. If you do this, you'll stay focused on development and be much more effective. As you ask this question and listen to God, He will give you some great insights and ideas.

I lead a ministry staff of twelve people. We meet weekly for training. I'd like to have a set curriculum for training in order to save preparation time, but it never works out that way for very long. When I ask myself and God, "What can I do to help my staff be more effective?" He gives me fresh ideas and insights. The set curriculum meetings are pretty good. But often when I ask the above question, I end up going off the plan and share something I sense God is telling me they need. They tell me those times are the most effective times we have.

Train them the way you wish someone else had trained you or did train you.

Maybe no one trained you to be a small group leader or to train leaders and you're learning as you go. Make mental notes of several elements you wish someone had taught you. These may include:

- Skills you had to learn the hard way.
- What works best for you
- What you regret doing

Development is Worth It

Development is the process of cooperating with God by using every available resource to help another person become a multiplying small group leader. It's the essence of multiplying potential leaders. It *is* hard work. And it *is* worth it. When you know the people you've developed are leading healthy, growing, multiplying groups, you'll be glad you paid the price and so will they.

The Multiplying Leaders Development Worksheet

I meet with my potential leader(s) _____(day of the week)
at_____ (time of meeting).

True or False: I need to get a regular meeting time.

The resource(s) we are currently using are: (on-the-job training,
personal meetings, classroom experiences, group training seminars,
wasting time together, books, tapes, magazines, etc.)
The resource I need to take better advantage of would be:

The step of training development activity (model, mentor, motivate,
multiply) we're currently doing is _____ with _____
(what activity).

The role (discipler, coach, counselor, teacher, sponsor) I need to be
playing with my potential leader(s) is:

True of false: I need to ask my potential leader(s) what role they most
want or need me to play for them at this time.

Pray this question and listen for God's response:
"What can I do to help my potential leader(s) be better prepared to
lead a healthy, growing multiplying group?

The elements of training I want to be sure they receive from me are:

DEPLOY:

Deploy Them into Leadership

When we started our church I received a great deal of joy from the development of the four other young men who came with me. We'd spent a few years in training prior to planting the church and it was fun to release them as strong leaders and to go from one group to five groups in our first year.

It was an even greater joy several years later when one of them took another huge step as a leader. With a core group from our church, he planted a new church. I am proud to say, his new church has grown stronger in its first three years than ours did. I feel like a proud papa when I brag on how well his new church is doing.

Parents derive greater joy from their children's progress than they do from their own. The apostle John said this was true in the spiritual world as well when he wrote, "I have no greater joy than this, that my children walk in truth" (3 John 4). I believe this principle is especially true for the multiplying leader. We can derive greater joy when our apprentices lead well and multiply their lives than we do, even from our own ministry.

One of the primary goals of ministry is to raise up additional ministers. The challenge isn't to raise up more followers, or even more helpers, but more leaders. The task of a multiplying small group leader isn't complete until the leader's potential leaders are leading their own groups and sending out their own leaders. The first seven chapters of this book were written to take a multiplying leader to that point. This chapter is to help them finish the task.

No One Succeeds Every Time

> The eighth step for developing a new small group leader is deploying potential leaders into ministry.

Not every person we send out to lead will succeed. We live in an imperfect world and things don't always go as planned. Even the best disciple-makers fail in some of their disciple-making efforts. If you don't believe me, consider the fact that even Jesus Christ, the greatest disciple-maker, experienced the failure of one of the twelve. I'm sure Jesus did everything right, but Judas still chose to go in the wrong direction. Judas never became a multiplier.

We can control what *we* do to help others multiply. But we can't control what *others* do with what we give them. Over the years I've tried to develop dozens of potential leaders. I can say with great joy that many of the ones I've trained have gone on into multiplication and are making a huge impact. Probably a higher percentage of those I've trained have become good leaders but ineffective multipliers. Some have moved over into other ministries and are doing quite well. Sadly, a couple of those I trained have ceased leading. We can't control the choices of others.

Although there'll be some 'failures' along the way, I've come to believe it's wrong to send out potential leaders who don't have a reasonable chance to succeed. If they step out to lead and fail, the results are very damaging. First, it hurts them and reduces the likelihood they'll want to lead in the future. Second, it hurts those they lead, who may be embittered by a bad experience. Third, it hinders the reputation of the Lord. Therefore, we want to do all we can to ensure the highest possible chance for success.

I've discovered that three actions are vital in effectively deploying potential leaders into ministry. The rest of this chapter will address those three actions.

1. Set Them Up For Success

While we can't guarantee or control the success of another, we must do all we can to make sure they do succeed. In order to gauge the success potential of the new leaders you're sending out, there are several factors to consider. Below I give my "big eight."

Indicators for New Leader Readiness:

1. They've completed the small group leadership training class and practical assignments offered by our small groups pastor.
2. They've become effective in leading various parts of our group meeting, such as the icebreaker, the prayer time, or the ministry time.
3. They've been effective at on-the-job training. They've displayed success at performing most of the eight habits of an effective leader, including prayer for group members, inviting new people, and contacting group members.
4. They have and use a good personal growth plan.
5. They have at least one good apprentice.
6. They have several people who are happy to follow their leadership in a new group.
7. They have a good place for the new group to meet. Preferably, they've secured a good host/hostess.
8. They have a good day and time for the new group to meet.

It's ideal to be able to put a big check mark by each of these eight indicators. Obviously, the more indicators they have in place, the greater will be their odds of success. As I look back over our ministry, those leaders with the most indicators have enjoyed the most success.

In the last several years, I've turned out some apprentices who failed to maintain a healthy growing group. One was great at teaching and leading various elements of the group meeting, but was lacking in the other key indicators. He had no apprentice, and wasn't sure where or when to meet. He struggled to maintain a growth plan. He rarely contacted or prayed for group members, or invited new people. I should never have sent him out. But I did and he failed.

Another failure involved a married couple with six indicators in place. But they picked a poor time to meet and hadn't proven to be successful at inviting new people. When one of their seed couples moved away, they were left with just themselves and their apprentice couple. And, after a year of struggling, they closed the group.

As you mentor your apprentices, let this checklist serve as a guide for things to consider as you help them move through the development process. Try to have as many indicators as strongly in place as possible before you send them out. If there are gaps before they're sent out, they rarely get filled in after they're leading.

Fill in the gaps first. If it means you send out fewer leaders, that's all right. It's better to send out a few really good ones than a lot of weak ones. The good ones will lead healthy, growing groups that multiply. The weak ones will probably close their groups before long, if they even get them going at all.

2. Send Them Out

As you prepare to send them out, be sure that not only the new leaders, but also the new group, are ready to survive the birth and succeed. While there are several ineffective ways to birth new groups, there's no one right way to do it. Any form of these three basic methods can be very effective, as can a combination of them.

Multiply: Two groups of equal size multiply from the parent group.

The vision of multiplication is shared. A new leader and/or leadership team develops. Relationships are developed. The group separates into two different groups for the prayer time. Group members are given the option of staying with the original leaders or being a part of the new group. The goal is to have a nearly equal amount of folks committed to both groups. For example, a group of sixteen adults multiplies into two groups of eight.

Launch: Core group from parent group launch new group.

As in option one, the vision of multiplication is shared. A new leadership team develops. Group members are given the option of staying with the original leaders or being a part of the new group. However, having equal numbers isn't necessarily the goal. The new leaders understand that the new group will be launched without many folks from the parent group. For example, a group of sixteen sends out a leadership team and others, totaling five adults to form a new group.

Plant: One person from the parent group plants a new group while others remain as a part of the parent group.

The planter is usually the original leader. For example, a women's group of eight sends out a highly committed, trained, experienced, and skilled leader to plant a new group on another day of the week. She's done it before. She knows several ladies who'll probably come and her apprentice is ready to take over her 'old' group.

We coordinate our church around three small group seasons: Fall (September, October, November, December); Winter (January, February,

March, April); and Summer (May, June July, August.). We use one Sunday morning celebration at the beginning of each season to enlist all church attendees into groups. This is the natural time for us to start most new groups. We find the best time to launch and plant groups is Fall. For us, the best time to multiply is usually January.[1]

Multiplying Suggestions

Part of setting up for success is preparing the group for its eventual multiplication. There are several ways to do this effectively.

Talk about multiplying early and often.
Start the very first week. Describe the fact that one of the purposes of the group is to raise up leaders who'll be sent out to lead new groups. At least monthly, pray in the group about the new groups to be birthed from this group. Keep the group informed of the plans and progress each step along the way.

Talk about multiplying in positive terms.
Don't speak of "breaking up" the group, "splitting" the group, or "dividing" the group. Instead talk about 'birthing" new groups, "launching" new groups, "multiplying" new groups, and "raising up" new groups and leaders. Your choice of words is important and powerful.

Talk about multiplying in terms of the big picture.
In our metropolitan area, there are over 850,000 unchurched people. More than 200,000 people live within convenient driving distance of our weekend worship services. Every new group that's born lowers the number of unchurched people. When we talk about birthing new groups, we talk about reaching more of the 850,000 people who are unchurched.

Our church has about two thousand members. Every new group creates a place for new folks to be incorporated into the family.

I find that when we begin to speak of multiplying, people often resist. Then we ask how many of them weren't in church or our group a year ago. This is usually over ninety percent. Then we ask, "What if the people who were in our group a year ago had been unwilling to give up their place in this group? Where would you be now?"

Pray about the best method and the best timing for
multiplying.

It's possible to make the right decision at the wrong time. Maybe the group is ready to multiply, but the new leaders are not. Or maybe the new leaders are ready, but the group is not. Or maybe it's a poor season to launch. For us, summer is usually not a good season to launch. Pray about finding the best timing for the multiplication.

Set a date for multiplying.

Setting a date for multiplying is essential in achieving the dream of multiplying your group. According to Joel Comiskey's survey of 700 multiplying cell leaders, he states:

> "Cell leaders who know their goal—when their groups will give birth—consistently multiply their groups more often than leaders who don't know. In fact, if a cell leader fails to set goals the cell members can clearly remember, he has about a 50-50 chance of multiplying his cell. But if the leader set goals, the chance of multiplying increases to three of four."[2]

Celebrate the new birth.

The Old Testament is full of God's command to celebrate momentous occasions with a feast. So, it's very appropriate to celebrate the birth of the new group with a party. What a joy it is to celebrate a new birth!

Plan a celebration with lots of food and invite guests. Ask your small groups pastor to oversee the evening. This may be a great time for testimonies. People who are staying with the original leader can share what the new leaders have meant to them. Those going with the new leader can share what they're hoping God will do through them and the new group. The small groups pastor will want to recognize the mentoring leader and will want to lead the group in prayer for the new leaders.

If your church doesn't have one already, you may want to work with your pastor on holding a commissioning service for new leaders. This is a powerful testimony of support for new leaders. A small group commissioning service is a time to recognize God's call on the life of the new leaders for this time. It's a chance to give public recognition and support for the task they're accepting. It's an opportunity to ask for God's special anointing on their new responsibility.

Such a service would involve recognizing the new leaders by name. You might want to also recognize the other members of the new group. The service would include having the new leaders come before the group or the church and praying for and over them. The senior pastor or small groups pastor might offer the prayer. Or each of the mentoring leaders could pray for the new leaders they've mentored.

The prayer should be for God's anointing on their new responsibility and the new group and asking God to protect them and their family. It would ask God to give the group growth, health, and multiplication. It would thank God for the many lives to be touched through the ministry of the group and these leaders.

The service could include giving each new leader a gift. A good book on leadership or small groups may be a nice gift. Or maybe the gift would be a subscription to a small group ministry magazine, or a gift certificate to a local Christian bookstore or a good restaurant.

The commissioning service could be a separate service or a part of another service. It could occur before the whole church or just before the other small group leaders. If your church isn't open to this sort of thing, that's not a problem. Simply make it a part of your final group time before the launch of the new group.

3. Stay in Touch

Parenting adult children is a high wire act of staying in touch, being available to help, and yet staying out of the way. In the same way, when you mentor a new leader it's easy to go to one of two extremes. Either you get too involved with the new group and leader, or not involved enough. Successful deployment requires the right amount of involvement and freedom.

Some of us have an "out of sight, out of mind" mentality. This is not what new leaders need. They need the mentoring leader to be available to listen, advise, encourage, and support them. The new leader needs the mentoring leader to serve as group coach unless there's another coach available. Several ways in which a mentoring leader serves as a coach to the new leaders include:

Contact them weekly for the first few months.
It's helpful if the mentoring leader calls the new leader weekly the first few weeks after the new group has begun, in order to see how it's going and talk through any issues.

Call on the new group meeting a time or two in the first few months.

Let the new leader know in advance and drop in on the group session. Remember that you're a guest, not the leader. Be highly supportive of the new leader and how God is using the new group.

Continue to pray for them regularly.

They need your prayers now more than ever. Ask God to give them wisdom and grace in leading the new group.

Celebrate every success the new group experiences.

Don't be jealous of their success or competitive with the new group leaders. In a sense, their success is your success. Let their success thrill your soul.

Challenge new leaders to keep the dream of multiplication before their new group.

It's easy for new leaders to be so focused on the health and growth of the new group that they lose sight of the dream of multiplication. Gently remind them of the dream. Speak to them of how they're working with their apprentices in preparing them to multiply other new groups.

Consult on any issues in which the new leader may seek advice.

Don't give advice that's not asked for, but do be ready to offer it when requested. Don't be a know-it-all, but on the other hand, don't be afraid to share what God has taught you through your experience.

The goal is the independence of the new leaders. They need to be able to lead without you. This means keeping your distance so they can grow and develop on their own.

The best way to learn to stay out of the way is to do it as you develop them. What I mean is when they're relatively new apprentices and you give them a portion of the group meeting to lead, like the icebreaker, let them do it. Don't jump in and correct or amplify, or edit everything they say. If there are adjustments or corrections you'd make to the way they did the icebreaker, save your comments until after the group. While they're leading, stay out the way. Otherwise, they'll never learn. If you selected good potential leaders, they'll surprise you with how well they lead.

Barriers to Deployment

An unhealthy "need to be needed"

Often leaders need to get over the need to be needed. Initially it may feel good for your ego if they're highly dependent on you. But you'll never multiply until they're no longer dependent on you. And ultimately, for an emotionally healthy leader, it will do more for your ego if you're multiplying leaders than it would if you never multiply because you have to do it all yourself.

An obsessive desire to have it done "right"

Some leaders get caught in the fallacy that there's only one right way to do something—their way. Actually there's usually more than one way to effectively handle the various aspects of leading a group. In fact, the way your apprentice wants to do it may be a better way than the way you always do it. Be open to learning a better way.

Everyone has a unique personality. Others need to do ministry in the way that fits their personality, not yours, and it may be very different than the way you do it. It will be more effective than if they did it your way.

Failing to take the time or make the effort to get others involved

Sometimes I've failed to give pieces of ministry away simply because it's easier to just do it myself. Taking the time and making the effort to prepare someone else to do it will initially take longer than just doing it myself. But, if I always do it myself, the apprentice will never learn how to do it.

A confused understanding of servanthood and humility

Some leaders never ask their apprentices to do anything because they mistakenly think that to do so shows a lack of being a servant or pride. However, it actually shows more humility to understand that you don't have to do it yourself. And it actually serves the apprentices more to give them a chance than it would to do it all yourself.

A Sweet Bitterness

Good parents build toward and brace themselves for the day their son or daughter heads off to college. It's a sweet bitterness because your relationship will never be the same. Good parents work so hard to help their children develop independence, but dread that moment at the same time. It's such a joy to see them get married, but it's sad as well.

There's a similar sadness involved in deploying people in whom you've heavily invested. You probably won't see them as often because both of you will be investing in new apprentices. But it's a sweet bitterness. The job has been accomplished. A new group leader has been deployed and a new group birthed. It's also a glorious sweetness because the Kingdom of God is being advanced and the church of Jesus Christ is being built. May you know this wonderful bittersweetness many times in your ministry life.

The Multiplying Leader's Deployment Worksheet

1. I've effectively set my potential leader(s) up for success:
__ Yes
__ No
__ Not yet, but I will

In order to do this I must:

2. I've planned to effectively send out the new leader(s):
__ Yes
__ No
__ Not yet, but I will

In order to do this, I will:

3. I've practiced staying out of the way all through the development process:
__ Yes
__ No
__ Not yet, but I will

In order to do this, I will:

Putting It All Together

As I've taught the eight essentials for multiplying leaders, the response is usually the same. People are excited and ready to go. But they look at it all and ask, "How will I find the time to do all this?"

Inspiration and information without application leads to frustration. This may be the most important chapter in this book because it helps you apply what you've learned to your life. You've learned eight essentials for multiplying leaders. Now that you know the essentials, and how to do them, the challenge is putting it all together. How can you apply all you've learned? How will you find the time to become a multiplying leader?

The essentials for multiplying leaders are several discernible steps of action. Multiplying leaders will need to work their way through each step

> The multiplying leaders keeps taking potential leaders to the next step of progress.

with each leader they mentor. They'll keep taking the next step toward the ultimate goal of effective group multiplication. They'll use prayer, advice from their coach, and this book to help them know and take the necessary small steps that make up each big step of progress.

In order to best discern your progress, I suggest using a Multiplication Progress Chart like the one shown below, or make your own. You'll find it an invaluable aid in multiplying leaders.

Multiplication Progress Chart

Date Step is Completed	Next Step to be Taken	My Next Step of Action
Being Prayerfully Considered:	Discovered as a Potential Leader	
Discovered:	Relationship Deepened	
Relationship Deepened:	Vision Described	
Vision Described:	Commitments Determined	
Committments Determined:	Leadership Developed	
Leadership Developed:	Deployed Successfully into Small Group Leadership	
Deployed Successfully into Small Group Leadership:	Goal: Have multiplied their group by:	

Potential Leader:

The key to applying the essentials for multiplying leadership is knowing and taking the next step and all the little steps in between. The sample given below shows a typical one-year progression of group member John Smith becoming a group leader. The leader just keeps pushing on to the next step. I've found that leaders who plan the next step do them successfully. Those who don't plan the next step don't train effective small group leaders.

Multiplication Progress Chart
(Sample)

Potential Leader: **John Smith**

Date Step is Completed	Next Step to be Taken	My Next Step of Action
Being Prayerfully Considered: Sept. 2002	Discovered as a Potential Leader	*Sept.- Pray for John daily until I'm clear on whether or not he's the one.* *Ask John and Susan to set up our fall group activity.*
Discovered: Sept./Oct. 2002	Relationship Deepened	*Mid Sept.- Have John and Susan over for dinner.* *Oct.- Be sure and call John weekly.* *Mid Oct. Take John and Susan to ball game.*

Date Step is Completed	Next Step to be Taken	My Next Step of Action
Relationship Deepened: Oct. 2002	Vision Described	*Mid Oct.- Ask John to lunch in order to share the vision.* *-In group, be sure to share the vision of multiplying our group.*
Vision Described: Nov. 2002	Commitments Determined	*Prepare copy of Eight Habits and small group leader covenant for John.* *- Set up weekly Sunday evening training session for us to meet together.*
Commitments Determined: Dec. 2002	Leadership Developed	*Jan.- Have John share his testimony with the group.* *- Have John begin to pray daily and call weekly the people who may potentially be in his new group.* *Feb.- Train John to lead the icebreaker.* *- Hold John accountable for personal growth plan.* *March- Discuss with John the possibility of the Jones' as possible apprentices for John's new group.* *- Train John to lead the prayer time each week.*

Date Step is Completed	Next Step to be Taken	My Next Step of Action
	Leadership Developed	*-Make sure John and Susan are signed up for small group training at the church.* *April- Begin to train John to lead the Bible discussion.* *-Coach John in how to approach the Brown's as host home couple for John's group.* *-Pray with John about multi-plication date.* *May- Announce multiplica-tion to the new group.* *Aug- Go with John and Susan to training seminar at the church.*
Leadership Developed: Jan. 2003 - Aug. 2003	Deployed Successfully into Small Group Leadership	*June-Aug.- Intentionally prepare group members for the multiplication of our group and John's new group.* *-Schedule our Small Groups Pastor to hold our commissioning serv-ice for John and Susan.*
Deployed Successfully into Small Group Leadership: Sept. 2003	Goal: Have multiplied their group by: Sept. 2004	*I need to stay in touch and out of the way in helping John lead, grow, and multiply his group.*

Taking the time to chart every potential apprentice is time well spent. It allows you to be able to tell at a glance where you've been, where you are and where you need to go next. Also, after you've effectively trained a few apprentices, the charts become handy guides for what to do with new leaders.

The challenge in multiplying leaders is staying focused. Most leaders get bogged down leading the group and lose sight of multiplication. Having a chart is a great way to stay on task. It's a great tool for small groups pastors or coaches to use with their leaders to help them stay on task.

Maybe you can come up with a better chart. Great! The best chart is the one you'll use.

In a few weeks, our high school group is scheduled to multiply. The new leadership team is getting ready. The location is determined. The multiplication party is being planned. The list of students who'll be members of the new group is being finalized. The new group is being listed in our updated church groups catalogue. We're anticipating a healthy multiplication from one healthy group to two.

I must admit I have mixed emotions. I'll be sad to not see the members of the new group as often. I'll miss being a more direct influence in their lives. I have doubts. What if they're not ready? I also have a couple of regrets. Why didn't I do more of this? If only I'd done more of that.

But when I really think about it, I'm simply filled with joy. My ministry is multiplying. The sum impact and attendance of the two groups will soon be greater than of the one. A new leader and new apprentices are stepping up and stepping out in the great adventure of leading groups. They're excited and afraid all at once. They're going to do a great job.

I pray that, if you haven't already, you'll one day know the joy, fulfillment, and satisfaction I'm experiencing as I watch our group multiply. I hope this book will help you successfully get to that day.

END NOTES:

Introduction:

[1] George Barna, *Leaders on Leadership* (Ventura, CA: Regal Books, 1997), 18.
[2] Quoted in Joel Comiskey, *Leadership Explosion* (Houston, TX: Touch Publications, 2000), 14 .
[3] Russ Robinson & Bill Donahue, *Building a Church of Small Groups*, (Grand Rapids, MI: Zondervan, 2001), 122-123.
[4] Joel Comiskey, *Leadership Explosion*,16.

Chapter 1:

[1] Joel Comiskey, *Groups of 12*, (Houston, TX: TOUCH Publications, 1999), 37.
[2] Betty L. Skinner, DAWS: *A Man Who Trusted God*, (Grand Rapids, MI, The Zondervan Corporation, 1974), 158.
[3] Ibid., 250.
[4] Ibid., 303.
[5] Ibid., 265.
[6] Ibid., 378.
[7] Ibid., 384.
[8] Paul Yonggi Cho, *Successful Home Cell Groups*, (Plainfield: Logos International, 1981), 168.
[9] Ibid., 168.
[10] George Barna, *Leaders on Leadership*, 48.
[11] Ibid., 51.
[12] Leroy Eims, *The Lost Art of Disciple Making*, (Grand Rapids, MI: Zondervan Publishing, 1980), 9.
[13] Walter A. Henrichsen, *Disciples Are Made - Not Born*, (Wheaton, IL: Victor Books, 1979), 143.
[14] Gene Warr, *You Can Make Disciples*, (Waco, TX: Word Books, 1978), 35.
[15] Waylon B. Moore, *Multiplying Disciples*, (Colorado Springs, CO: NavPress, 1981), 5.
[16] Ibid., 30.
[17] Ibid., 16.
[18] Ibid., 112.

Chapter 2:

[1] Peggy Anderson (Editor), *Great Quotes for Great Leaders*, (Franklin Lakes, NJ: Career Press, 1997), 35.
[2] Waylon B. Moore, *Multiplying Disciples*, 10.
[3] Ibid., 112.
[4] Joel Comiskey, *Groups of 12*, 34.
[5] Peggy Anderson (Editor), *Great Quotes for Great Leaders*, 13.
[6] Randall Neighbour, *Answers To Your Cell Group Questions*, (Houston, TX: TOUCH Publications, 2000), 31.
[7] Ibid., 33.
[8] Paul Yonggi Cho, *Prayer: Key To Revival*, (Waco TX: Word Books, 1984), 15.
[9] Ibid., 18.
[10] Ibid., 19.
[11] Ibid., 12.
[12] Joel Comiskey, *Home Cell Group Explosion*, (Houston, TX: TOUCH Publications, 1998), 26.
[13] Joel Comiskey, *Leadership Explosion*, 34.
[14] Peggy Anderson (Editor), *Great Quotes for Great Leaders*, 43.
[15] George Barna, *The Power of Vision*, (Ventura, CA: Regal Books, 1992), 29.
[16] Joel Comiskey, *Home Cell Group Explosion,* 15.

Chapter 3:
[1] Russ Robinson & Bill Donahue, *Building a Church of Small Groups*, 126.
[2] Joel Comiskey, *Leadership Explosion*, 35.
[3] Joel Comiskey, *Groups of 12*, 65.
[4] Russ Robinson & Bill Donahue, *Building a Church of Small Groups*, 127.
[5] Jim Collins, *Good To Great*, (New York, NY: Harper Collins Publishers Inc., 2001), 41.
[6] John C. Maxwell, *Developing the Leaders Around You*, (Nashville, TN: Thomas Nelson, 1995), 38.
[7] Paul Yonggi Cho, *Successful Home Cell Groups*, 111-112.
[8] John C. Maxwell, *Developing the Leaders Around You*, 47-60.
[9] John Maxwell and Jim Dornan, *Becoming a Person of Influence*, (Nashville, TN: Thomas Nelson, 1997), 129.
[10] John C. Maxwell, *Developing the Leaders Around You*, 38.

Chapter 4:
[1] John Maxwell and Jim Dornan, *Becoming a Person of Influence*, p. 79.
[2] Ibid., 81.

Chapter 5:
[1] George Barna, *Leaders on Leadership*, 48-49.
[2] Paul Yonggi Cho, *Successful Home Cell Groups*, 168.
[3] Alan Loy McGinnis, *Bringing Out the Best in People*, (Minneapolis, MN: Augsburg Publishing House, 1985), 18.
[4] George Barna, *Leadership Explosion*, 54.
[5] Ibid., 47.
[6] Ibid., 49.
[7] Ibid., 48.
[8] Ibid., 55.
[9] George Barna, *The Power of Vision*, 19.
[10] George Barna, *Leadership Explosion*, 56-57.
[11] Paul Yonggi Cho, *Successful Home Cell Groups*, 171.
[12] Ibid., 170.
[13] George Barna, *Leadership Explosion*, 57.
[14] Ibid., 57.
[15] Larry Stockstill, *The Cell Church*, (Ventura, CA: Regal Books, 1998), 53.

Chapter 6:
[1] Leroy Eims, *Be the Leader You Were Meant To Be*, (Wheaton, IL: Victor Books, 1975), 55.
[2] John Maxwell and Jim Dornan, *Becoming a Person of Influence*, 139.
[3] Joel Comiskey, *Home Cell Group Explosion*, 29

Chapter 7
[1] Joel Comiskey, *Leadership Explosion*, p. 39.

Chapter 8
[1] Dave Earley, *8 Habits of Effective Small Group Leaders*, (Houston, TX: Touch Publications, 2001), 74-75.
[2] Joel Comiskey, *Home Cell Group Explosion*, 46.
[3] Dave Earley, *8 Habits of Effective Small Group Leaders*, 76-77.

ADDITIONAL CELL GROUP RESOURCES

HOW TO LEAD A GREAT CELL GROUP MEETING . . .
. . . So People Want to Come Back by Joel Comiskey

Joel Comiskey takes you beyond theory and into the "practical tips of the trade" that will make your cell group gathering vibrant! This hands-on guide covers all you need to know, from basic how-to's of getting the conversation started to practical strategies for dynamic ministry times. If you're looking to find out what really makes a cell group meeting great . . . this book has the answers! 144 pgs.

LEADING FROM THE HEART, by Michael Mack

Recharge your cell leadership! Powerful cell leaders share a common trait: a passionate heart for God. They know their priorities and know that time with Him is always at the top of the list.

Do your cell leaders attract others? Is their cell ministry central to their lives? This book will renew their hearts, refocus their priorities and recharge their ministry.

If you have a sense that your leaders are tired of ministry or frustrated with people, this title will help! And, if your leaders have great attitudes and you want to help them move to the next level, this book will move them into new fields, white for harvest!

8 HABITS OF EFFECTIVE SMALL GROUP LEADERS
by Dave Earley

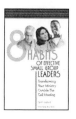

Are your cell leaders truly effective in changing lives? They can be! After years of leading and overseeing growing small groups, Pastor Dave Earley has identified 8 core habits of effective leaders. When adopted, these habits will transform your leadership too. The habits include: Dreaming • Prayer • Invitations • Contact Preparation • Mentoring • Fellowship • Growth. When your leaders adopt and practice these habits, your groups will move from once-a-week meetings to an exciting lifestyle of ministry to one another and the lost! 144 pgs.

ANSWERS TO YOUR CELL GROUP QUESTIONS,
by Randall G. Neighbour

As your cell leaders face new challenges, it's comforting to know there's a resource they can turn to when they need answers to specific questions and issues. *"Answers to Your Cell Group Questions"* covers the entire gamut of cell life and leadership and is written by Randall Neighbour, a seasoned cell leader and President of TOUCH Outreach Ministries.

This book is an invaluable resource for you and your leaders! Topics include: working with difficult or hurting people, how to facilitate a meeting the right way, working with children, training interns and releasing the ministry to them, jump-starting a cell group that doesn't care about the lost, etc.

ADDITIONAL CELL GROUP RESOURCES

LIFE IN HIS BODY, *by David Finnell*
Communicate the vision of the cells to everyone in your church
with this simple tool. The short chapters followed by discussion
questions clearly define cell life for your leaders and members so
that they can catch a lifestyle of prayer, community and
evangelism. This book will give your church hope and vision as
your members discover the possibilities of the New Testament
community. 160 pgs.

UPWARD, INWARD, OUTWARD, FORWARD WORKBOOK
Improving the 4 Dynamics of Your Cell Group, *by Jim Egli*
You can now take your cell leaders and interns through the same
strategic planning workshop TOUCH® offers across the country!
   This easy to use workbook, combined with the facilitator's
presentation (a FREE download from our website) will help your
cell groups grow in the four basic dynamics of healthy cell life.
Upward: Deepening your relationship to the Father; Inward:
Deepening community between cell members; Outward:
Reaching the lost for Jesus successfully; Forward: Developing
and releasing new leaders. 72 page student workbook

303 ICEBREAKERS:
At last . . . 303 ways to really "BREAK THE ICE"
in your cell group! You will never need another icebreaker book.
This collection places at your fingertips easy-to-find ideas divided
into nine categories, such as "Including the Children," "When a
Visitor Arrives" and "Lighthearted and Fun." This is a needed
reference for every cell meeting. We've included instructions on
how to lead this part of the meeting effectively. 156 pgs.

OUR BLESSING LIST POSTER
Growing cell churches have proven that constant prayer for the lost
yields incredible results! Use this nifty poster to list the names of
your *oikos* and pray for them every time you meet. 34" x 22", folds
down to 8.5" x 11" and comes with a handout master, equipping
track and a master prayer list. Pack of 10.

ARE YOU FISHING WITH A NET?
by Randall G. Neighbour
Lead your group into team evangelism. These proven steps will
prepare your members to reach out effectively as a group. 12 pgs.

Make Cell Groups Work Online!

Our website was designed for pastors just like you!

Free articles from *CellChurch Magazine* & *CellGroup Journal.*

Fast and secure online resource purchases.

Watch a streaming video on the cell movement.

Discover other churches with cell groups in your area or denomination.

Post your resume or search for a new staff member in our cell-based classifieds area.

Free downloads of leader's guides, presentations, and software to track cell growth.

Interact with other pastors and experts in our bulletin board forum.

What are you waiting for?

Grab a cup of coffee and visit us now...

www.cellgrouppeople.com

ADDITIONAL CELL GROUP RESOURCES

CELL GROUP LEADER TRAINING:
by Scott Boren and Don Tillman

The *Trainer's Guide* and *Participant's Manual* parallel the teaching of Comiskey's *How to Lead a Great Cell Group Meeting*. Through the use of teaching, creative activities, small group interaction, and suggested between-the-training exercises, this eight-session training will prepare people for cell group leadership like no other tool. The *Trainer's Guide* provides teaching outlines for all eight sessions and options for organizing the training, including different weekly options and retreat options. The *Trainer's Guide* also has bonus sections, including teaching outlines for the *Upward, Inward, Outward, Forward* Seminar and detailed interview discussion guides for *The Journey Guide for Cell Group Leaders*. This comprehensive training tool will establish your group leaders on a sure foundation.

HOW TO BE A GREAT CELL GROUP COACH
by Joel Comiskey

Research has proven that the greatest contributor to cell group success is the quality of coaching provided for cell group leaders. Following in the footsteps of his bestselling book, *How to Lead a GREAT Cell Group Meeting,* author and church consultant Joel Comiskey provides a comprehensive guide for coaching cell group leaders. Chapters include: What a Coach Does, Listening, Celebrating, Caring, Strategizing, Challenging, and more. This book will prepare your coaches to be great mentors, supporters, and guides to the cell group leaders they oversee.

MAKING CELL GROUPS WORK AND THE NAVIGATION GUIDE
by M. Scott Boren, Bill Beckham, Joel Comiskey, Ralph Neighbour, Jr., and Randall G. Neighbour

These resources break down the transition process into eight manageable parts. If your church is just beginning its transition, these materials will help you focus on building cells on a sure foundation. If you are in the midst of developing cell groups, it highlights where to focus your energy. No matter where you are with your church, these resources will help you identify your current stage of cell development and articulate a plan to address that stage.

THE JOURNEY GUIDE FOR CELL GROUP LEADERS

This tool will help your interns and cell leaders evaluate their leadership abilities and determine their next steps toward effective group leadership. It will help you as a pastor or trainer identify the needs of your future or current leaders so that you can better train and mentor them.